TALES FROM
ANCIENT
EGYPT

Cover photograph: a 30th Dynasty "Scribe of the Gold" on a re-used block from the tomb of Neferseshem-Psamtik, discovered at Memphis by Mariette in 1860, now in Cairo Museum (JE 10978).

TALES FROM ANCIENT EGYPT

BY

JOYCE TYLDESLEY

RUTHERFORD PRESS

First published in Great Britain in 2004
Rutherford Press Limited, 37 Rutherford Drive, Bolton, BL5 1DJ
Registered Office: 52 Chorley New Road, Bolton, BL1 4AP

www.rutherfordpress.co.uk

A CIP catalogue record of this book is available from the British Library

ISBN 0-9547622-0-7

Printed and bound in Great Britain by Biddles Ltd, King's Lynn

CONTENTS

CHRONOLOGICAL TABLE

3000 BC	**Archaic Period** Dynasties 1-2	Unification of Egypt Foundation of Memphis Royal tombs at Abydos
2500 BC	**Old Kingdom** Dynasties 3-6	Djoser's Step Pyramid at Sakkara Khufu's Great Pyramid at Giza
2000 BC	**First Intermediate Period** Dynasties 7-11(early)	Collapse of royal rule
	Middle Kingdom Dynasties 11(late)-13	Theban kings reunify Egypt Arts and literature flourish
	Second Intermediate Period Dynasties 14-17	Hyksos rule at Avaris
1500 BC	**New Kingdom** Dynasties 18-20	Theban kings reunify Egypt Tuthmosis III Amarna Period Ramesses II
1000 BC	**Third Intermediate Period** Dynasties 21-25	Northern kings at Tanis High Priests of Amen rule at Thebes
500 BC	**Late Period** Dynasties 26-31	Egyptian royal dynasties interspersed with periods of foreign domination
	Ptolemaic Period	Alexander the Great
31 BC		

EGYPT AND HER NEIGHBOURS

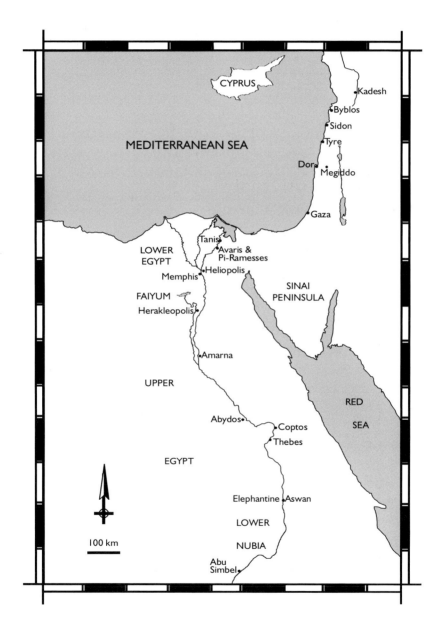

CYPRUS

Kadesh

Byblos

Sidon

MEDITERRANEAN SEA

Tyre

Dor

Megiddo

Gaza

Tanis

LOWER
EGYPT

Avaris &
Pi-Ramesses

Heliopolis

Memphis

SINAI
PENINSULA

FAIYUM

Herakleopolis

Amarna

UPPER

RED

SEA

Abydos

Coptos

Thebes

EGYPT

Elephantine Aswan

LOWER

100 km

NUBIA

Abu
Simbel

INTRODUCTION

*While the Writer was at work in the shade of the first pylon, an
Arab storyteller took possession of that opposite doorway, and
entertained the donkey-boys and sailors. Well-paid with a little
tobacco and a few copper piastres, he went on for hours, his shrill
chant rising every now and again to a quavering scream. He was
a wizened, grizzled old fellow, miserably poor and tattered; but
he had the Arabian Nights and hundreds of other tales by
heart.*

Amelia B. Edwards, *A Thousand Miles up the Nile*, 1877

Did the Ancient Egyptians enjoy listening to stories? It seems
almost inconceivable that they did not. In the absence of
pubs, theatres and, of course, television, we can easily envisage
convivial dark evenings enjoyed around a comforting fire; the
whole family sipping sweet beer and listening spellbound as the
local storyteller spins his yarns. Even easier is it for us to picture an
Egyptian mother telling her sleepy children a much-loved folktale
handed down from her own mother and grandmother. Although
we have no direct evidence to support these cosy imaginings, the
fictional Papyrus Westcar (here retold as *Five Magical Tales*) lends

some confirmation to our cheerful fireside scene by telling us how the real Old Kingdom court of King Khufu, the most cosmopolitan and sophisticated court of its time, was entertained by a series of stories told - not read - by the royal princes.

We will never know how many Egyptian tales were told and retold but never written down although, in a society where only an estimated one - ten percent of the population was literate, it seems reasonable to assume that most people heard stories rather than read them. We do know that some stories were written down because, while the vast majority of Egypt's writings have been lost in the mud-brick ruins of her houses, palaces and offices, a few have beaten the odds and survived in the dry desert tombs or on the stone temple walls. Occasionally we can even catch a fleeting glimpse of the men who copied the stories down; a brief endnote attached to *The Shipwrecked Sailor*, for example, tells us that it was written by the scribe Amen-aa, son of Ameny, although this does not mean that Amen-aa was the original author of the work.

We can guess that the more official stories, those committed to stone, were compiled by scribes working under elite patronage, while the less formal tales preserved on papyrus either belonged to private libraries, or were copied by tutors anxious to provide their students with lengthy texts which they themselves could copy. And we can further speculate that these stories, both the fiction and the true-life autobiographies and adventures, were primarily intended to be enjoyed by the elite - more specifically, the educated male elite. The stories that entertained the lower classes may well have completely disappeared because no-one wrote them down.

So where are the surviving stories now? While the myths and legends of the classical world have passed into general circulation and blockbuster films, the stories of Ancient Egypt, undeniably the world's most "popular" and intensely studied ancient culture, remain stubbornly confined to dense academic publications and to footnotes in learned journals. These stories - complex, vibrant, dark tales of creation, death, sex, violence, friendship and betrayal -

deserve to be read and enjoyed by a new audience. The primary intention of this book is simply to entertain the reader by allowing a brief insight into another, long-lost world. But if reading these stories and their accompanying commentaries brings some under-standing of the lives and thoughts of their anonymous authors - and how could it fail to? - so much the better.

I have chosen to retell the stories rather than provide a straight translation of the surviving texts. Precise translations are, of course, fundamental to our understanding of Egyptian literature, and there are many excellent translations recommended in the Bibliography and Further Reading that ends this book. But strict translations bring their own problems for the non-specialist reader.

First come the intricate scholarly arguments over the exact meaning of individual words that interrupt the narrative flow and force translators to ornament their text with copious footnotes.

When all queries are resolved we are left with a false air of accu-racy. A translation, however diligently prepared, can only ever be one person's interpretation of a given sequence of words; anyone who doubts this should compare the various versions of the same tales cited in the Bibliography - all the stories are essentially the same, yet all are subtly (and in some cases not so subtly) different.

The conscientious translator must seek accuracy above all, but words and plot are not the only, or even the most important, aspect of storytelling. The feel of a story is equally dependent upon its style, and it is the style of a piece, and our instinctive recognition of and response to that style, that allows us to hear the author's true voice. Unfortunately, modern readers are condemned to read ancient stories through the thick filtering blanket of our own cul-tural experience. This is unavoidable; we cannot hope to approach the stories in the same frame of mind as their original audiences.

Finally, and perhaps most importantly, a precise translation can bring a false sense of completeness, petrifying a tale that once enjoyed a more fluid telling. This is a dilemma that the Egyptians themselves well understood. To preserve a story on paper, or papyrus, or to carve it in stone, is to freeze that one version, giving it a validity which it may not deserve. In Egypt, where written words had magical properties, this effect was magnified. Anything committed to writing became a form of truth. This could, of course, be a good thing. When Ramesses II wrote of his victorious campaign against the Hittites he ensured that his own highly biased account would become official Egyptian history. It is just Ramesses's bad luck that we are also able to read the very different Hittite report of the same battle. In modern times committing a story to film can have a similar freezing effect. Few, having seen the cartoon version of Cinderella, remember the dark folktale that preceded it. Fewer still realise that Cinderella, in the original, was equipped with a sensible warm slipper of *vair* (fur) rather than *verre* (infinitely more uncomfortable glass) - a translator's error that has now irretrievably become part of the Cinderella legend. Thanks to Disney, the Cinderella story has almost ceased to evolve.

This brings us to some unanswerable questions. Egyptian literature uses archaic language and short, staccato sentences, but is this really how the stories were performed? Would the storyteller have quoted word for word from a text, or would he have embellished the bare bones, lingering over certain aspects, hurrying over others, but always telling the same essential tale? Would he have recited his tale, chanted it, acted it or even sung it, perhaps with percussion accompaniment in the style of modern, nomadic storytellers?

Writing appeared in Egypt at the beginning of the Dynastic age. The first preserved writings are bureaucratic lists closely linked to funerary rituals; we have details of goods to be included in tombs, offerings to be made to the deceased, and titles to be preserved for eternity. By the end of the Old Kingdom this repetitive and essentially dull repertoire had evolved to include lengthy autobiographies and intricate spells or prayers for the dead. Functional writing had taken its first steps towards imaginative literature, yet was still very much sealed in the dark tomb. Didactic texts - secular instructions or teachings written primarily to educate but also to entertain the living - soon followed. But it was not until the Middle Kingdom, a time of great artistic and cultural development, that stories as we know them today were first written down. This book includes tales stretching over at least two thousand years of literature from the early Middle Kingdom *The Shipwrecked Sailor* to Plutarch's version of *The Tale of Isis and Osiris*.

How were the stories written down? The earliest Egyptian writings used hieroglyphics; a non-alphabetic script made up of three types of sign (phonograms, logograms and determinatives) arranged in rows or columns, and read from either left to right or right to left. Hieroglyphs, with their elaborate drawings of birds, fish and flowers, were beautiful to behold but complex and time-consuming to write. Five hundred years later, at the start of the 2nd Dynasty, the hieratic script was developed to meet the needs of the growing bureaucracy. Hieratic is an abbreviated, speedier, version of hieroglyphic script that requires the harassed scribe to make fewer pen-strokes. It is always read from right to left. While temples, tombs and official inscriptions continued to employ the traditional hieroglyphs, papyri and ostraca (fragments of pottery and stone used as notepads) were henceforth written in hieratic. It is curiously touching, one of those rare moments of total empathy with the peoples of the past, to see just how often the neat handwriting of the lengthier papyri deteriorates into a hieratic scrawl as the weary scribe nears the end of his work.

I have divided the book into thematic sections, each telling a very different type of story, and every story is followed by a brief commentary that sets it in its chronological and cultural context. The Four Tales of Gods are myths - stories that venture into a long-vanished divine past to offer fantastic explanations for things that cannot otherwise be explained. Where did we come from? Where do we go when we die? How does the sun travel cross the sky? And where does it go at night? They are both the science and history of the ancient world, although they are not necessarily expected to reveal one literal truth. As such they can have no definitive version and no sole or named author. Myths start in the oral tradition and evolve with time and the growing understanding of the rhythms of life. So we find, to take just one simple example, that the myths associated with Horus in the Archaic period classify him as the strong falcon god of kingship, sun and sky and are very different from the myths associated with the same god in the Graeco-Roman period when he is better appreciated as the divine infant born to Isis and Osiris.

The Seven Tales of Men come closer to our own understanding of narrative fiction. They are plot-driven stories that set out to entertain rather than explain, although they may include a less than subtle message for the reader: Egypt is the best country in the world; Egyptian justice will invariably triumph; pharaoh is the son of a god; eloquence is always a good thing. Primarily based in the human rather than the divine world, and occasionally including real people alongside fictional companions, they tell of the deeds and misdeeds of invented heroes, never heroines. Good women rarely leave the security of the hearth to feature in formal Egyptian literature, while their bad sisters make the briefest of appearances in order to confirm the worst prejudices of their authors before disappearing in suitably horrific fashion. These stories place their heroes in exotic settings - in strange lands, or the distant past - and only the lengthy *Talkative Peasant* remains firmly rooted in the humdrum, everyday world. The original audience would have found elements of these stories highly amusing - the Egyptians were fond of elaborate wordplay, irony and, at the other end of the comedy spectrum, crude, almost slapstick humour. Jokes were used both to entertain and to make serious points. Unfortunately this is one aspect of their culture that is almost impossible for us to recapture.

The Four True Stories are almost exactly what their title suggests; true-life tales of intrepid exploration and magnificent battles preserved by Egypt's male elite. Real "Boys' Own" reading these, the battle scenes at least require a certain suspension of disbelief from the modern reader. The two private texts, an autobiography and an official report, tell of foreign travel and trade in exotic goods, an important, but often overlooked, aspect of Egypt's foreign policy. We should not expect scrupulous self-awareness from these personal histories; the "warts and all" approach had absolutely no appeal to the ancient Egyptian. In the case of Wenamen, we cannot even confirm that his story is a true one. Fact or fiction - perhaps it does not matter over-much. Wenamen's tale, like that of Harkhuf, reveals a wealth of accidental detail and makes fascinating reading.

The extravagant victories described by the New Kingdom monarchs Tuthmosis III (18th Dynasty) and Ramesses II (19th Dynasty) show us the opposite, official and unashamedly aggressive side of Egypt's foreign relations. From the very beginning of the Dynastic age it had been understood that the Egyptian king should take every available opportunity to smite the miserable foreigners who cringed at his borders, threatening to disrupt the order of his land. Advances in military technology at the beginning of the New Kingdom, including the advent of the light horse-drawn chariot and the powerful composite bow, facilitated this ambition. Battles were welcomed as an opportunity for glory; it was quite simply unthinkable that Egypt, backed by her superior gods, might lose.

The final section, One Hymn, is a simple retelling of *The Great Hymn to the Aten*, the long, mystical poem preserved in the tomb of the courtier Ay at the sun-worshipping city of Amarna. As it was never intended to be a work of fiction, and has very little plot, it could be argued that this piece has no place in a self-confessed collection of entertaining stories. But the beauty of the language, and the obvious sincerity of the author, transcend time and translation to make *The Great Hymn* a compelling read and a suitable ending to this book.

FOUR TALES OF GODS

The average Egyptian was never dismayed by inconsistencies in religious matters: he seemed rather to be fascinated by them.

Donald Mackenzie, *Egyptian Myth and Legend*, 1913

1

THE CREATION OF THE WORLD

In the beginning nothing existed but the terrible, swirling waters
of chaos. There was no land and there was no sky. No gods, no
people, no light, no warmth, no time and no death. Only the dangerous, endless waters. But deep within that dark sea there floated
a perfect egg. And trapped within that egg was a solitary spark of
life which struggled constantly to escape.

Suddenly, inexplicably, the egg cracked open beneath the waters.
Life broke free of its confining shell, and the dark sea felt its birth
and was mightily disturbed. With an almighty roar, and a great
surge of foam, an earthen mound rose out of the waters of chaos.
Seated on that mound was the all-powerful being Atum.

Atum had created himself, and he laughed out loud in his triumph. He shone as the sun and brought light to his new world.
Now he set about creating the living. Grasping his penis he masturbated and, while he masturbated, he spat and he sneezed. From the
fluids of his body emerged twin children, Shu the god of the dry
air and his sister-wife Tefnut, goddess of moisture. And Atum and
Shu and Tefnut lived safe on their island-mound in the midst of the
dark sea of chaos.

Atum loved the twins. They meant everything to him. They
brought him great happiness, but also a painful anxiety that
clutched at his heart and clouded his vision. For they were innocent
and naive, and he worried about them day and night. He could not

bear to let them out of his sight lest some unrecognised evil should befall them. But one dreadful day he did look away, just for a moment. It was long enough. Shu and Tefnut wandered away from his protection and fell into the sea of chaos. Shrieking and calling to their father for help, they disappeared beneath the waves. And Atum stood on his island and watched his children go. Atum was alone again.

Distraught, and blinded by his tears, Atum summoned his Eye to search for his lost children. The Eye of Atum looked long and hard, scanning the waters with her powerful gaze. At last she found the twins bobbing about in the depths of the dark sea. As she restored Shu and Tefnut to their father, Atum's tears of grief turned to tears of joy. Copious, they fell to the ground. And from these tears sprang men and women. From this time on, mortals and immortals would live in harmony on the mound.

Tefnut gave birth to twins; Geb the handsome god of the earth and Nut the beautiful goddess of the sky. Geb lay down and became the fertile land. He bore the fields and the marshes and the great River Nile. Grain sprouted from his ribs, and plants from his back. His laughter brought earthquakes, and his anger brought famine. Nut loved her splendid brother and happily bore his children, the glittering stars that decorated the dark night sky.

Then one day a terrible thing happened. The ever-hungry Nut swallowed her children whole. Geb flew into a furious rage and the land trembled and shook with his wrath. To escape Geb's anger Nut spread her arms and legs and stretched herself above her brother, her fingers and toes resting on the horizons of the north, east, south and west. And Shu stood between his beloved children, holding them apart lest they should continue their violent quarrel.

Now Nut's arched body separated the world from chaos. Her laughter brought thunder and her tears brought rain. Along her body the stars and moon twinkled at night. And every evening she swallowed the sun so that it passed, hidden, through her body to be re-born from her womb at dawn.

COMMENTARY ON
THE CREATION OF THE WORLD

The world's great monotheistic religions each draw their theology from a single sacred book offering one, uncontested, tale of creation. The Egyptians, generously polytheistic and lacking anything approaching a divine revelation, embraced a wide variety of creation myths. Some of these appear very strange to modern eyes. Depending on where and when an Egyptian lived, he might understand that his world had been created by the self-generated god Atum or by the self-generated god Re, that it had started with the emergence of a huge scarab beetle from the petals of a beautiful lotus flower, or even that it had hatched from a monster-sized egg laid by a gigantic celestial goose. Local creation myths starred local gods, so the intellectual earth god Ptah spoke the mysterious word that created life at Memphis while 600 miles away on the island of Elephantine, Khnum the craftsman was kept busy moulding mankind on his potter's wheel. Contradictory though they appear to modern eyes, these stories were accepted as having equal validity - they were just slightly different ways of explaining the same thing. Akhenaten's ill-fated Amarna experiment excepted, there was never any attempt to force an official theology on the people.

Atum's story is the ancient creation myth of the priesthood of Heliopolis, the followers of the sun god. It is drawn from a jumble of references in the Old Kingdom Pyramid Texts, the Middle Kingdom Coffin Texts, and the New Kingdom Book of the Dead, and it features the immensely powerful god Atum, Lord of Totality. Atum usually takes the form of man wearing the double crown of Upper and Lower Egypt, although he can also be represented as a snake, a scarab beetle, a ram-headed man and, more rarely, as a lion, ichneumon, bull, lizard, ape and even as the mound of creation itself. His name, meaning "finish" or "complete", emphasises his dangerous dual nature. Atum has the ability to create everything and in so doing, ultimately, to finalise or end everything.

His is a creation myth rooted in the observation of the natural world. The land emerges from the swirling waters of chaos just as Egypt herself re-emerged every year from the dark red waters of the receding Nile floods. As the Egyptians well knew, this "new" land would be moist and fertile, yielding a crop that would be the envy of the ancient world. The idea of the life-giving primeval mound was echoed in the raised mounds that covered even the most basic of Egyptian graves; with its mound in place the grave became not only a symbol of death, but a promise of resurrection for the deceased. Eventually the grave-mound would evolve into the pyramid, a recognised powerhouse of rebirth for kings and their queens. Mounds could be found in formal temple architecture too, with the floor rising gradually as the priest moved from temple door to inner sanctuary.

The world - Egypt - emerges from uncontrollable chaos. The conflict between chaos (*isfet*) and order (*maat*) is fundamental to the Egyptian way of thinking, and a recurrent theme in all Egypt's tales. Chaos is simple for us to understand, threatening as it so often does, to engulf our own lives. *Maat* is a far more nebulous concept; the opposite of chaos it is variously and with equal validity translated as "rightness", "status quo", "control", "order" and "justice". *Maat* may also be personified in the form of the goddess Maat, a beautiful woman who wears the feather of truth on her head. At all times chaos lapped around the edges of the well-ordered Egyptian world. It was fear of this chaos that prevented the Egyptians from experimenting with their traditions - if things were done as they had always been done, there was little danger of upsetting *maat*. To pharaoh alone fell the awesome responsibility of holding back *isfet*. For without firm control, deprived of *maat*, Egypt would surely fail. And, with all time ended, the world would sink without trace to be lost again beneath the dark waters. Only Atum and Osiris, god of the dead, would survive such a catastrophe by taking the form of gigantic snakes.

Here the creation of mankind is of very little interest, occurring as it does almost by accident as a by-product of Atum's tears (a deliberate play on words, as the Egyptian word for tear sounds like the word for men). It is the creation of the land and its gods that really matters. Egypt's deities are never too lofty to indulge in the most basic of human practices. As the one and only self-created being, Atum has no choice but to mate with himself to reproduce. The hand that he uses to masturbate becomes representative of his own female element, so that Atum and his hand effectively become a couple, while the goddess Iusaas, worshipped at Heliopolis, is interpreted as a personification of the same divine hand. Queens of Egypt will later bear the uncompromising title "God's Hand" in direct reference to their own role in physically stimulating both the semi-divine pharaoh and his gods.

Atum has become the father and mother of the gods and of mankind. His children, Shu (literally "emptiness"; the god of air, clouds, mist and light) and Tefnut (the enigmatic goddess of dampness or moisture, whose name has no literal translation), reproduce in incestuous union, as do their children and their grandchildren. Of course, they have little choice in this matter - there is a distinct shortage of eligible partners at the beginning of the world. But in so doing they set a fashion for royal incest. Brother-sister and father-daughter marriages link the royal family to the gods, while setting them apart from the commoners who show little taste for such close unions. No one, it seems, royal or not, was tempted by a mother-son marriage. In practical terms incestuous royal marriages made good sense. They ensured that the queen, as well as the king, could be trained to her duties from birth. More importantly, the exclusion of outsiders from the innermost royal circle restricted the number of potential claimants to the Egyptian throne.

Geb, the son born to Shu and Tefnut, was an ancient earth god who represented both the fertile land and the graves dug deep into that land. For this combination of attributes, and for his prowess as a healer, he was both respected and feared. Geb usually appears as a man, often reclining beneath the female sky, and his naked body is often painted green to denote his impressive fertility.

Nut, his sister-wife, is both a beautiful woman and the celestial cow or sow that arches herself above Geb, separating the world from the ever-threatening sea of chaos. Sows occasionally eat their young. Every night Nut swallows the sun, which is reborn every morning; every morning she swallows the stars that are reborn every night. As a goddess of rebirth Nut appears on the under surface of countless coffin lids, so that the dead lie directly beneath her outstretched body and, if the coffin is understood to represent Nut, are themselves reborn directly from her dark womb. They appear in many tombs, but neither Geb nor Nut had a specific cult centre.

Although his cult would soon be overshadowed by the cult of Re of Heliopolis, Atum would remain a powerful being to the end of the Dynastic age. Atum and Re were essentially elements of the same solar deity whose combined characteristics found expression in the one god Re-Atum. While Re-Horakhty (a fusion of Re and the falcon god Horus) was celebrated as the young and vigorous morning sun, Re-Atum became the old and tired evening sun.

2

THE DESTRUCTION OF MANKIND

King Re had ruled Egypt for many, many years. He had ruled wisely and well, and gods and mortals had flourished under his guidance. The seasons had developed a dependable rhythm. The fields were green, the river teemed with fish, and the deserts glittered with flecks of gold. Presiding in the law courts Re had guaranteed justice for both the living and the dead. Writing in the sacred books he had recorded the rituals that would protect Egypt from chaos until the very end of time. Everything should have been perfect. But mankind had grown vain and dissatisfied and, ill concealed in the desert, rebels were daring to plot against their king. Re was already an old man. His bones were turned to silver and his flesh to gold, although his hair was still as dark as lapis lazuli. And with old age came the old man's intolerance of fools. Re's heart was weary. He was beginning to think about leaving the ungrateful world of the living and plunging back into the primordial waters of creation. But before he could decide his own fate he had to deal with the blasphemies of mankind. He wanted a quick solution to his problems.

Re summoned his fellow gods to a secret council away from the prying eyes of mortals. Late that night Shu and Tefnut, Geb and Nut, and Nun the primal mound, and all their retinues, slipped quietly into the palace. They crept to the king's private chamber and stood in respectful silence on either side of his great golden throne.

With them came Re's beloved daughter Hathor, the gentle comfort of her father's old age.

The gods bowed low before their lord in greeting. Then with great courtesy Nun invited Re to speak, so that they might learn of his troubles and help him. Re spoke with dignity, but he could not hide his anger.

"Mankind, who grew from my tears, is plotting against me. I am surrounded by treachery and can trust no one. Even now, as I speak to you, rebels are foolishly attempting to hide from me in the desert. They think that they are cunning, but of course I can see them all. I know their darkest thoughts, and I know what they hope to achieve. Again and again I think of ending my misery by killing them, each and every one. But I will not do this until I have your approval. Tell me what you would do in my place."

Hearing this unhappy tale, stern Nun gave his opinion. Mankind was indeed ungrateful and deserved to die. The time had come for Re to release the fury hidden deep within his quiet daughter. Hathor must transform into the vengeful Eye of Re.

And so it was done. Soon the desert ran red with blood as the Eye of Re hunted down the traitors who threatened her father and killed them, one by one. Merciless, immune to sobs and pleadings, she turned her burning gaze on the rebels. She did not stop until they were all dead and the sands were littered with bodies. Then, temporarily satisfied, she licked her lips and returned in triumph to her father.

Re welcomed Hathor back with joy and gratitude, but his happiness was tempered with apprehension. For Re belatedly realised the true power of the force he had unleashed in his dutiful daughter. The sight of so much killing had sickened him, and he had decided that the rest of mankind should be spared. But Hathor, the Eye of Re, had tasted human blood and liked it. She was unstoppable. She had become fierce Sekhmet the fiery destroyer, and she could not be swayed from her mission to slaughter all of mankind.

Re thought long and hard, and at last devised a plan to thwart his obsessed daughter. Sending for his swiftest messengers he ordered them to seek out vast quantities of red ochre. The ochre was to be brought in sacks to Heliopolis, where it would be ground to finest powder by his most trusted servant, the High Priest of Re. At the same time scores of serving maids would be put to work grinding many hundreds of baskets of grain. The grain was to be used to brew seven thousand jars of beer, and the red pigment was to be stirred into the beer, turning it blood red. And so Re's plan was put into operation.

The dark day came when Hathor-Sekhmet, the vengeful Eye of Re, planned to destroy the rest of mankind. But King Re had risen early that day, and had travelled to the killing fields ahead of her. Here he had emptied the seven thousand jars of red beer so that the fields were flooded to a great depth. The Eye of Re saw the foaming red liquid covering the land and, believing it to be human blood, rejoiced that her task was so easily accomplished. She bent down low, saw her own beautiful face reflected in the red beer, and was entranced.

Hathor-Sekhmet had a great thirst. She drank the red beer - all seven thousand jars worth - and, as her vision blurred, grew dazed and confused. She lay down and slept for many hours in the fields. That night she returned home to her father satisfied, and never realised that she had failed to destroy mankind.

Re should have been happy. The rebels were dead, mankind was saved, and Hathor was once again his gentle daughter. Life could return to normal. But Re's heart was sorely troubled. He could not forget what he had seen and heard. He found it impossible to forgive mankind's ingratitude, and he no longer wished to rule on earth. Re appointed his trusted grandson Geb as his heir. Then, leaving his fellow gods behind, Re clambered onto the back of the celestial cow and rose into the heavens. From this lofty vantage point he was able to watch mankind still quarrelling beneath him.

COMMENTARY ON
THE DESTRUCTION OF MANKIND

The Destruction of Mankind forms the opening section of a text known as the *Book of the Cow of Heaven* which is not literally a book, but a collection of magic spells preserved in varying degrees of completeness on the walls and furnishings of the tombs of Tutankhamen, Seti I, Ramesses II, Ramesses III and Ramesses VI in the Valley of the Kings, Thebes. This gives the story a firm New Kingdom context, although linguists believe that it was composed during the Middle Kingdom. Its theme, the inherently evil nature of mankind, is a timeless, universal and often-repeated one recognisable to all readers. Here we are taken back to the very beginning of Egyptian history, to the time when Egypt was ruled by gods. Modern readers may have difficulty in accepting divine kings but the Egyptians did not; both The Turin Canon of Kings (a papyrus history of early Egypt) and the historian Manetho (writing for Ptolemy II) include the god-kings on their lists of Egypt's rulers.

By the 4th Dynasty the cult of Re had displaced the cult of Atum as Egypt's principal solar rite. This made very little difference to anyone. The name of the god may have changed, but his nature had not, and the most fervent prayers were still directed towards the all-powerful sun who, disappearing every night, offered the threat of eternal darkness. It would be difficult for us to overstate the importance of sun worship during the Old Kingdom. Re was revered throughout Egypt, but his magnificent temple, or Great Shrine, was situated at a site today best known by its Greek name Heliopolis, or "Sun City". Known to the ancients as Iunu, Heliopolis now lies buried beneath a suburb of modern Cairo.

Although the Great Shrine no longer exists, throughout Egypt surviving pyramids, sun temples and obelisks all testify to the importance of solar symbolism in formal architecture. Re would survive the disruptions of the Intermediate Periods, and gain renewed influence during the New Kingdom as one element of the mighty god of the Egyptian empire, Amen-Re.

Like Atum before him, the divine Re is a self-generated solar being credited with creating the world. His version of the creation story differs little from the one we have already read. Emerging from the waters of chaos Re slashes his penis to release two children, Hu and Sia, from his own dripping blood. He then remains to rule on earth until, growing old and tired, he retreats to the heavens. Every day he pilots his solar boat across the sky, assisted by a divine crew that includes his daughter Maat and the spirits of the dead pharaohs. Every evening he transfers to his night boat and descends to make a dangerous journey through the despair of the underworld. Here in the darkness his loyal crew will help him by defeating Apophis, a fearsome serpent daemon who attacks Re every night.

Safe within their earthly temple, a roofless building open to the sky, the priests of Heliopolis also help Re by performing the hourly rituals which will ensure that the sun will be reborn safely. Their obsession with the passing of time led to the development of the northern calendar; a year of twelve months of varying length with, as the year averaged only 354 days, an occasional thirteenth month added. Meanwhile, in southern Egypt a rival lunar calendar based on the rising of Sothis (Sirius, the Dog Star) was in use. Following Egypt's unification the two calendars were merged into one civil calendar. The year was now divided into three seasons (inundation, winter and summer) of four months of thirty days. An extra five days gave the necessary 365, but there was no leap year. Slowly the official seasons slipped out of sync with the actual seasons and with the old lunar calendar, which had been retained by the priesthood. Only every 1,456 years, when the civil New Year's Day coincided with the traditional New Year's Day, did matters correct themselves.

Re can take many guises, although he is usually shown as a winged sun disk, as a falcon, or as man with the head of a falcon, a ram or a beetle. The sun shining in the sky represents both Re himself and the benign Eye of Re, his daughter-wife Hathor. Hathor, Lady of Perfume, is a daughter full of womanly charm and is widely celebrated as a goddess of motherhood, sensuousness, music and healing. In some tales she assumes the role of the Golden One to accompany Re on his daily journey across the sky. In others she is the gentle cow who suckles the King of Egypt. At Memphis she is the Mistress of the Sycamore who sustains the dead with food and drink; at Thebes she is the compassionate Mistress of the West who cares for the dying sun. But when she is roused, mild-mannered Hathor transforms into Sekhmet, The Powerful One. Sekhmet is an uncompromising lion-headed goddess who breathes fire and who is armed with plagues and pestilence. She works to protect Egypt's kings and is known to strike fear into the heart of Egypt's enemies.

By now Re is firmly associated with kingship, and all pharaohs are officially recognised as "Sons of Re". Re's earthly reign is a golden age when mortals and gods live together. This is the Egyptian equivalent of the Garden of Eden and life should be idyllic but, as in the Bible story, mankind is not content with his lot. Politics has raised its ugly head and, for no apparent reason, the people are rebelling against their king. It may simply be that Re is considered too old to rule effectively. Egypt has a horror of aged and infirm kings, and will require every long-standing pharaoh to reaffirm his ability to rule by completing the *heb-sed* or jubilee rituals every thirty years. Re, like all of Egypt's gods, is not immortal; he ages, and is sensitive and vulnerable to the attacks of mankind. His response, simple but effective, is to wipe out mankind and start again.

Parallels with Biblical, Mesopotamian and Greek tales of

destruction are obvious. Here the slaughter starts not with a flood - in Egypt, land of the annual inundation, floods are considered beneficial - but with the rampaging Eye who burns her enemies with the merciless heat of the sun. Observing the carnage but not necessarily swayed by the plight of one specific individual (there is no Egyptian equivalent of Noah and his family), Re changes his mind. Again we are not told why, although it is possible that he has recognised that the elimination of mankind will effectively eliminate the hourly offerings made in his earthly temples. Whatever his reasoning, he hatches a devious plot to halt his daughter's indiscriminate slaughter.

Hathor is known to have an unquenchable thirst - along with her more refined female attributes, she is also celebrated as the goddess of drunkenness. Beer was a staple of the Egyptian diet quaffed by men, women and children at all meals and offered to the gods in daily rituals. Sweet and soupy, and so thick that it was often drunk through a filtering straw, it was nowhere near as strong as modern beers. As brewing was a home-based industry inextricably linked with baking, it was classed as a female skill. For a long time Egyptologists believed that the Egyptians made their beer from partially fermented, lightly baked bread. However, experimental archaeology indicates that the beer is far more likely to have been made from malted grain, an assumption that is supported by occasional finds of sprouted cereal in domestic contexts.

The story ends with Re's ascent into heaven. This, given the text's strong funerary association, may be equated with the rebirth and ascension of the dead pharaoh.

3

THE TALE OF ISIS AND OSIRIS

Nut bore Geb two divine sons, Osiris and Seth, and two divine daughters, Isis and Nephthys. Osiris, her first-born son, was a happy, sunny baby. He was all that a mother could wish for. At the time of his birth the people rejoiced throughout the land that a future king had been born. But his brother Seth was troubled and angry, and his birth caused Nut great pain as her unruly son forced his way into the world through her side. Old King Re had already passed into the skies, leaving Geb to rule Egypt. This he did wisely and well for many years. And when the time came for Geb to hand on his crown he overlooked the clever but unpredictable Seth, and chose Osiris as his heir and successor.

Seated on his golden throne Osiris ruled Egypt as a caring and just king, his modest sister-wife Isis beside him. Egypt flourished and grew civilised under their rule. King Osiris rescued mankind from its savage state; he taught the men how to plant crops, obey laws and worship the gods. Queen Isis, who was as wise as she was beautiful, taught women the secrets of weaving, baking and brewing. Later, with Egypt at peace, Osiris left Isis to rule on his behalf as he travelled the whole world, beguiling the people of many nations with his fluent speeches, his songs and his poetry.

One person, however, was deeply unhappy, his heart eaten up with jealousy, rage, and a growing hatred of his family. For Seth, who had so longed to be King of Egypt, was forced to stand by and watch as his good but essentially dull brother ruled in his place. While Osiris received the love and respect of the people he, the brilliant and charming Seth, was entirely overlooked.

Brilliant he may have been, but Seth was fatally flawed. He was prepared to think what should have been unthinkable. He had determined that his brother must die so that he might take his place. While Osiris was away on his travels he managed to hide his discontent behind a smiling face, for he knew that the all-seeing Isis was watching him. But when Osiris returned home Seth realised that his time had come. He recruited seventy-two evil men as his co-conspirators, and started to plan his brother's murder.

Seth planned a magnificent banquet. The food stands were piled high with joints of beef and mutton. There was every kind of fowl and fish, pyramids of bread and sweet honey cakes, the freshest of vegetables and heaps of succulent fruit. And to wash it all down there were jars of finest wine and copious quantities of strong beer. The air was perfumed by exotic incense mingled with the scent of many bouquets of flowers. And to add to the enjoyment, entrancingly beautiful women played sensual music on flutes and harps, while their equally beautiful sisters danced, oiled and half-naked, in the flickering lamplight. Never had there been such a party.

Seth had invited his seventy-two new best friends to the banquet, but the guest of honour was Osiris, King of Egypt. The guests ate and drank then ate again until they could not consume another morsel. Sated, they sat back on their stools and sipped their drinks. Finally, when Seth judged that enough wine had been consumed, he signalled to his servants, and a long, narrow chest was dragged into the centre of the banqueting chamber. The chest was a beautiful piece of work. Carved by a master-craftsman from the finest wood, it was inlaid with bands of gold and silver and decorated inside and out with ebony, ivory and precious stone. The guests fell silent, and marvelled before the chest.

Seth spoke. The chest was a party game - the climax of the

evening's entertainment. Whoever could lie down inside the chest could keep it. It was a most valuable prize indeed. There was a scramble as Seth's allies rushed forward and attempted to squeeze their bulky bodies into the narrow space. But none fitted. Then the slender Osiris, his perceptions blunted by the wine, stepped forward to take his turn. He lay down in the chest. It was a perfect fit, as Seth knew it would be - he had secretly measured his brother's body weeks before. But before Osiris could sit up to claim his prize Seth slammed the lid shut and shot the bolt home. The splendid chest, tailored exactly to Osiris's measurements, had become his coffin.

The party was over. Abruptly dismissing his guests, Seth coated the coffin in lead then dragged it to the mouth of the Nile and threw it in. Caught by the tide, the coffin slowly sailed northwards into the great sea. Seth laughed out loud as he watched his brother bob slowly out of sight. With Osiris dead and vanished, he could now claim the throne of Egypt. And these dark events happened in the twenty-eighth year of Osiris's reign.

News of the tragedy spread, and eventually reached Isis in her palace at Coptos. Sorrowfully, the queen unbound her hair and assumed mourning clothes as a mark of respect for her husband.

Now Seth was King of Egypt, and life resumed its normal rhythms. But, refusing to forget Osiris, Isis spent many years wandering the length and breadth of Egypt hoping to find news of her vanished husband. Eventually she heard a rumour that the precious wooden chest had been washed ashore in the faraway land of Byblos. Here it had lain against a lovely young cypress tree, which had grown to envelop the chest so that Osiris, sealed in his coffin, was completely hidden within its trunk. Eventually the cypress tree had been cut down, and used to hold up the roof in the great pillared hall of the palace of the King of Byblos.

Isis made her way to the palace of Byblos, where she sat next to a splendid fountain in the palace gardens, and wept bitter tears of despair. Here the queen's serving maids found her, and spoke kindly to her. And Isis, putting aside her sorrow, braided their hair and perfumed their skin so that they appeared beautiful and smelled wonderful. When the Queen of Byblos saw her maids she wished to meet the woman who had effected such a transformation. So Isis was introduced to the Queen of Byblos, and became nursemaid to her younger son.

Isis loved the young prince, and cared for him dutifully by day. At night, when no one could see, she set him at the centre of a ring of immortal fire so that he might gain eternal life. She turned herself into a bird so that she might fly round and round the pillar that held Osiris. And as she flew around the pillar, she gave great cries of grief. Her cries woke the Queen of Byblos who rushed to the hall. Seeing Isis in the form of a bird, and her child in the midst of the flames, the queen gave a great scream of terror. This sudden noise broke the potent spell, denying her baby son the chance of immortality.

Isis regained human form and, very angry with the queen, demanded the pillar that housed the body of Osiris. Horrified, the queen agreed at once. Taking the pillar from beneath the roof Isis cut into its wood until the decorated chest was revealed. She discarded the remains of the pillar; these would be venerated forever in the temple of Isis at Byblos.

When she saw Osiris's coffin Isis let out an ear-piercing shriek; a shriek so loud that the younger son of the King and Queen of Byblos died from shock. Isis took the coffin, and the elder son of the king and queen, and placed them in a boat, and set sail for Egypt. For she wanted to bury her husband in his own land.

Isis landed in the bleak Egyptian desert. Believing herself to be all alone she opened up the coffin, threw herself on the body inside and wept copious tears. The young Prince of Byblos approached silently from behind, for he wanted to see what great treasure could be held in the ornate chest. But when he caught sight of Isis's face, he dropped dead from fright and Isis ran away.

Seth, out hunting alone in the moonlight, stumbled across the body of Osiris still lying in its coffin in the desert. He could hardly believe his eyes. Incandescent with rage, he hacked his dead brother into pieces and flung the fourteen body-parts far and wide. Thus he denied his brother a proper burial.

But he had reckoned without his determined sisters. Transforming themselves into birds Isis and Nephthys searched high and low, recovering the scattered parts until only the penis was missing. This would never be found, for the greedy Nile fish had eaten it. Isis, the divine healer, equipped her husband with a replica organ, bandaged him, then sang the spell that would bring him back to a semblance of life. Transforming herself once again into a bird, she hovered over her husband's restored body. Her magic was very powerful; nine months later she would bear Osiris a son.

Osiris was alive, but he was no longer a living king. He abandoned his family and retreated in sorrow to the Underworld where he would henceforth rule as King of the Dead. Isis was forced to flee with the baby Horus to the papyrus marshes. Here she protected him with her potent magic until he was old enough to claim his inheritance.

COMMENTARY ON
THE TALE OF ISIS AND OSIRIS

The elaborate story of Osiris and his sister-wife Isis is one of Egypt's most ancient tales, but it is best preserved in Greek, in Plutarch's masterpiece, *De Iside et Osiride*. Plutarch based his story on original Egyptian myths included in the writings of earlier classical writers, and dedicated it to the priestess Klea, a follower of the cult of Isis. His version, adapted to fit with traditional Egyptian accounts of the same myth, has been used as the basis of this retelling.

With the appearance of Osiris, Isis, Seth and Nephthys we finally meet all the gods of the Ennead - the nine deities (Atum and his direct descendants Shu, Tefnut, Geb, Nut, Osiris, Isis, Seth and Nephthys) who, in the sun-based Heliopolitan tradition, were the direct ancestors of Egypt's living kings. Osiris rose from obscure northern origins - possibly starting his career as a nameless daemon or a minor fertility god - to become one of the most important beings in the Egyptian pantheon. As his power and influence grew, he was able to usurp the myths and tales developed by other deities until he had accumulated a complete and complex mythology of his own. The story of his miraculous resurrection, for example, was almost certainly "borrowed" from the far more obscure cult of the god Andjety of Busiris. Unable to complete with his powerful appeal, the priests of Re absorbed the newcomer into their own cycle of tales, making Osiris a part of their own theology.

Later wisdom would maintain that Osiris had been born in the cemetery-desert just outside Memphis, but as King of the Dead he was primarily worshipped at the Delta site of Busiris, and at Abydos, cemetery of Egypt's most ancient kings and home to later royal cenotaphs. Other towns claimed an affiliation with his cult as sites where parts of the god's dismembered body had been recovered: the god's missing heart was apparently found at the Delta site of Athribis, while at least four towns put in rival claims to have housed a lost leg! No one was able to declare a link with the dead god's penis, as this most important member had been eaten by the rapacious Nile fish; henceforth, or so the classical authors believed, fish were avoided in Egypt as unclean animals. Archaeology reveals a different story, with vast quantities of Nile fish consumed by rich and poor alike throughout the Dynastic age.

Egyptian texts do not specifically state that Seth murdered Osiris; to commit such an atrocity to writing would presumably have strengthened its awful reality. But everyone knew exactly what had happened. Osiris quickly came to symbolise, jointly and severally, all of Egypt's dead kings. They, mummified like their new sovereign, were eternal kings in the shadowy Underworld while their successors, the Horus kings, ruled the living Egypt. A dead king, or King of the Dead, could have been an intensely threatening figure. And indeed, Osiris's appearance offered little in the way of reassurance to those frightened by the thought of their own mortality. Osiris was an uncompromising mummy - a white bandaged body whose folded arms held the crook and flail of kingship and whose unwrapped head was fitted with curled beard and wig or crown. But Osiris did not only symbolise death, he was also a god of rejuvenation, agriculture and the inundation, whose erect and unfeasibly large penis - occasionally depicted in funerary papyri - emphasised his role as a fertility god. Osiris's tragic story offered the hope of life beyond the grave - a hope that the life-loving Egyptians desperately sought. As Lord of the Living, the dead Osiris became one of the most popular gods in the Egyptian pantheon.

In Osiris's heavily bandaged body we have a mythological justification for the science of mummification. The Egyptians believed that the survival of the physical body was crucial to the survival of the soul beyond death. They knew that this was not an impossibility.

Although all meats rotted rapidly in the hot Egyptian sun, the ancient graves dug into the desert sands held bodies that, although shrunken and tanned, remained recognisably human even after many centuries. The deceased had been inadvertently preserved by their direct contact with the sterile sand, which leached moisture away from the decaying corpse. The problem was that wealthy Egyptians did not want to be buried in simple holes in the desert. They wanted coffins, and sarcophagi, and cool stone-lined tombs providing plenty of space for grave goods. They wanted to be separated forever from the preserving hot sands. And so a great deal of effort was put into developing a technology which would, as far as possible, replicate the natural drying effect of the desert. The final product - the stiff, bandaged mummy - converted the dead Egyptian into a convincing Osiris look-alike.

Isis is first named as a protective deity in the 5th Dynasty Pyramid Texts. As she grows in popularity she absorbs the traditions and accessories of many other goddesses including the once dominant Hathor, so that by the end of the Dynastic age Hathor and Isis are virtually indistinguishable in appearance. Isis is the ideal wife for Osiris. She is beautiful, wise and fertile. While things go according to plan, she remains modestly in the background, supporting her husband and attending to the domestic tasks that are traditionally the wife's lot. Yet we should not underestimate her. Isis is cunning and well-versed in magic, and she is quite capable of independent action should the need arise. It is she who poses the greatest threat to Seth's ambition. Her healing powers, in particular, are unsurpassed, magic being an important aspect of the Egyptian healer's training. While Osiris takes a sabbatical to travel the world it is Isis, and not Seth, who is left to rule in his absence; the tradition of the wife deputising for the husband is a well-documented one, and we have examples of Egyptian women from all walks of life directing their absent husbands' affairs.

The story of *Isis and the Seven Scorpions*, carved on the Late Period

Metternich Stela (housed in the Metropolitan Museum, New York), combines the two most important aspects of Isis's personality - her magical powers and her compassionate motherhood - in one brief tale. This story, which is included amongst a collection of healing spells, tells how Isis flees from Seth accompanied, as the tale's title suggests, by seven scorpions. They seek a night's lodging at the house of a rich woman but perhaps understandably, given the curious nature of the party, they are refused shelter. Taking refuge at the home of a poor but generous woman, they plot their revenge. Six of the scorpions lend their stings to the seventh, a scorpion named Tefen. Tefen scuttles into the house of the rich woman and stings her young son. Distraught, the woman runs round the village seeking help for her dying child, but no one comes to her aid. Just as she has rejected a plea for help, so her own pleas must go unanswered. Isis, of course, cannot allow an innocent boy to suffer for his mother's actions, so eventually she cures him by reciting the names of all seven scorpions. In Egypt, knowledge of a name conferred power, and yet a third tale tells us how Isis sets out to discover the name of the sun god so that she might dominate him. Meanwhile, in true storybook style, the rich woman realises the folly of her deeds and gives away her wealth.

Back in our main story, Isis gives birth to Horus, the son and heir who will protect his dead father's funerary cult. Isis and her son Horus symbolise all that is good and powerful about Egyptian motherhood. Their legend survived into the classical world, where images of Isis suckling Horus served as inspiration for early Christian artists seeking to depict the Virgin Mary and the infant Jesus.

There was one member of Osiris's immediate family who certainly did not conform to the ideal of family loyalty. Seth, the Red One, god of the infertile desert and lord of foreigners, was an ancient, discontented being. He symbolised confusion and disorder, and should perhaps have been a direct affront to the concept of *maat* and the maintenance of the status quo. Attempted fratricide/

regicide - Seth's worst offence - would have been anathema to the Egyptians who placed a high value on family loyalty and who regarded their kings as so far above their fellow Egyptians as to be untouchable. Yet Seth was no Satan. He was not shunned, or barred from the pantheon, but was accepted as a necessary complement to the extreme goodness and virtue of Osiris and Horus. And indeed, Seth was not all bad - it was he who helped Re to fight off the dreaded night-time serpent Apophis. Worshipped in the Delta town of Avaris, Seth, or Seti, gave his name to three New Kingdom pharaohs (Seti I, Seti II, and Sethnakht). His appearance typifies his confusing nature, as Seth's human body is topped with a curious animal-head, which was probably intended to be frightening, but which appears to modern eyes as an unfortunate combination of aardvark and long-eared pig or donkey.

Nephthys, the beautiful, shadowy wife of Seth, is the most elusive of the divine quartet, a funerary deity who protects the dead and supports her grieving sister Isis. Later tradition allows Nephthys a brief moment in the limelight; Plutarch tells us that she had an affair with her brother Osiris (Osiris, being blameless in this matter but perhaps somewhat short-sighted, had mistaken Nephthys for her sister) which led to the birth of the jackal-headed funerary god Anubis.

4

THE DISPUTE OF HORUS AND SETH

Safe in the shelter of the papyrus marshes, and protected by his loving mother, Horus grew into a wise and handsome young man. Eventually the time came for him to claim his inheritance. Horus left the marshes and travelled with Isis to testify before the council of the gods. Seated before the great throne of the Universal Lord, he formally requested the crown of his dead father Osiris. Unfortunately things did not go as Horus and Isis had expected, for Seth was not prepared to surrender his hard-won kingship lightly, and some of the gods were on his side. The legal quarrel between Horus and Seth was to last an amazing eighty years.

Shu spoke in favour of the fatherless boy. Surely it was right that Horus, son of Osiris, should be King of Egypt. Thoth the divine scribe agreed. "It is a million times right that he should be king."

On hearing this, Isis let out a great shriek. Running forward to stand before the great throne of the Universal Lord, she ordered the north wind to fly westwards and give the glad tidings to Osiris, isolated and sorrowing as he was in the Land of the Dead. But Isis had acted in haste, and the Universal Lord was not amused. He sat in silence, furious with the council. They had taken it upon themselves to pronounce judgement without waiting to hear his opinion, and he had been inclined to award the crown to Seth, son of Nut. For Seth was infinitely strong and cunning while Horus was an untried and untested boy.

Uncertain how to proceed, the Universal Lord sent for Banebdjedet, the great living god, so that he might judge between Horus and Seth and stop them quarrelling. For their dispute had already lasted for many years and everyone had grown weary of it. Banebdjedet duly presented himself before the council, but he declined to offer an opinion. The matter should not be decided in ignorant haste. A letter must be written to Neith, Mother of the Gods, asking her advice. She alone should decide between the rival kings. And so Thoth wrote an elaborate, diplomatic letter explaining matters to Neith.

"What shall we do with these two claimants who for eighty years now have been asking the council for a decision? No one wants to judge between the two. Write quickly, and tell us what we should do."

Neith replied briskly, in writing, and Thoth read out her judgement. The matter was clear cut. Horus was the rightful king, and any attempt to trick him out of his birthright would make Neith so angry that she would bring the sky crashing down. Horus should receive his father's throne, but Seth should receive suitable compensation, including Anath and Astarte, the beautiful daughters of the Universal Lord, as wives. The gods at once agreed, calling out to each other that of course the wise Neith was right. But the Universal Lord grew angry again, as the judgement had not gone the way he intended. Turning on Horus he hurled a childish insult at him:

"You are too feeble to be king and, what's more, your breath stinks".

This so incensed his fellow gods that they, too, started to insult each other. As the opinionated god Babi abused the Universal Lord, "No one cares what you think - you are a worthless god with no followers and your shrine is empty!", the council meeting degenerated into chaos and confusion and the Universal Lord stormed out.

The Universal Lord was so upset by the behaviour of the council that he retired to his tent where he lay sulking on his bed. After a long time his gentle daughter Hathor, Lady of the Sycamore, came to find him. Sensing his gloom, and wishing to cheer him up, she stripped off her clothes and stood naked before him. This made her father laugh out loud. Recovering his humour and his strength he left his tent and returned to the council of the gods. He had decided that Horus and Seth should each be allowed to plead his own case.

Seth spoke first. "I am Seth, son of Nut, and greatest in strength of all the gods. Every day I sail in the solar boat of Re, and every night I slay Apophis, the great serpent who threatens the life of the sun. No other god is able to do this. Therefore I should receive the crown of Osiris."

The gods were impressed by Seth's powerful speech, and divided amongst themselves. Some argued that Seth should indeed be king, but Thoth repeated the pertinent question. "Is it ever right that a brother should inherit when a dead father has left a living son?"

For the opposition Banebdjedet, no longer a neutral observer, argued that it was not right to overlook Seth in favour of his young nephew.

Then the Universal Lord spoke. But his words were not fit to be heard, and were not written down. All we know is that they outraged his fellow gods, who made a great outcry.

Next it was the turn of Horus, son of Isis, to speak. His message was simple and direct. "It is very bad indeed that you are defrauding me, and denying me my father's crown."

Hearing this, the passionate Isis could remain silent no longer. Furious, she swore an impressive oath: "By my mother, the wise goddess Neith, this matter should be brought before Atum of Heliopolis, and also before Khepri."

And the gods agreed with her that it should be so.

In a towering rage, Seth in turn swore an oath. "Upon my word,

I swear that I will take my heavy sceptre and kill one of you each and every day. But I will not go to court if Isis is allowed to be there."

The Universal Lord agreed that the over-emotional and rather irritating Isis should be kept out of the case. He felt that a change of scene would do everyone good and so he ordered that the gods should cross the water to the Isle-in-the-Midst, and there decide the matter. To ensure that they reached their decision undisturbed, he forbade the ferryman to transport any woman to the Isle. In particular, he banned any woman who looked even remotely like Isis. And so it was done. The gods crossed to the Isle and there they sat in the cool shade of the green trees to enjoy a hearty picnic.

Isis, great in magic, would not be thwarted. Turning herself into a bent old woman she hobbled up to the ferryman and pleaded for passage to the Isle.

"For I have brought a bowl of gruel for a hungry young lad who has been tending cattle on the Isle for five long days."

The simple ferryman was worried. This aged crone looked nothing like a beautiful goddess, but how could he be sure? He had been specifically told not to ferry any woman across the river. Finally he managed to stifle his doubts, and accepted Isis's valuable gold signet ring as payment for her passage.

Walking under the fragrant green trees of the Isle-in-the-Midst, Isis saw her fellow gods, Seth included, eating their meal in front of the splendid tent of the Universal Lord. And Seth looked up from his meal and saw Isis, but he did not recognise her, for she had transformed into a nubile maiden, the most beautiful girl in the whole land. Seth desired this gorgeous girl very much. He left his food, and walked quickly to intercept her, before the other gods could see her. Hiding behind a sycamore tree, he called out to Isis in what he considered to be an irresistibly seductive manner.

"Well, hello there, lovely lady. Here I stand waiting for you, most beautiful girl in the world. Let us walk and talk together in the shade of the tall green trees."

Isis replied in a whisper, her soft golden voice spinning a heart-rending tale.

"First let me tell you my story, stranger. I was once the wife of a herdsman. I loved him, and I bore him a son. We were a happy family. Then my husband died, and my young son began to look after his father's cattle. But a stranger came and took over my stable. The stranger threatened to beat my son, to confiscate his cattle, and evict him from his rightful home. Now, please sir, I would like you to give me your opinion on this matter."

Seth, moved almost to tears by the beautiful woman's plight, replied without thought.

"It can never be right to give a family's cattle to a stranger when the son of the dead father lives. The usurper should be beaten with a staff. He should be evicted from the stable at once, and your son should inherit his father's position."

On hearing Seth's words Isis transformed herself into a giant bird and flew to perch in the topmost branches of an acacia tree. She shrieked down to Seth in triumph.

"Weep for yourself, Seth, not for me. For you have condemned yourself with your own words."

Then Seth indeed began to weep, and he ran to the Universal Lord and cried before him, explaining all that had happened. The Lord listened with a grave face. Seth had condemned himself - what more was there to be said? But Seth demanded that the ferryman be brought before the gods and severely punished, for he had ignored the orders of the Universal Lord and had brought Isis to the Isle. And so the unfortunate ferryman was dragged before the council, and his toes were cut off in punishment. And from that day forward the ferryman hated the sight of gold.

The gods left the peace of the Isle-in-the-Midst and crossed the water to the Western Bank. Furious, and not prepared to admit defeat, Seth challenged his nephew to a duel. They would each transform into a hippopotamus, and dive to the deepest depths of the sea. They would stay underwater for three whole months.

If one of them should emerge before the appointed time, he would forfeit his right to the crown. Horus agreed, and into the swirling waters they plunged, side by side. But Isis, hearing of the challenge, sat on the shore and wept bitter tears. For she feared that Seth would kill her son.

Isis decided to help Horus. She took a length of flax and twisted it into a rope. Next she fetched an ingot of copper, melted it, and cast it in the form of a harpoon. She tied the rope to the harpoon, and threw it into the water at the point where Horus and Seth had vanished beneath the waves. Under the water the harpoon bit into the flank of Horus, who gave a loud shriek.

"Help me mother! Tell your barb to let me go, for I am your son, Horus."

Isis ordered her harpoon to release Horus, and threw it again into the water. This time it bit into the flesh of her brother, and it was Seth's turn to give a loud wail.

"What harm have I ever done to you, Isis? I am your brother, yet you hate me more than you would hate a complete stranger."

Hearing his words Isis was greatly moved and once again she commanded her harpoon to release its victim.

Horus interpreted his mother's mercy as a betrayal, and was enraged. He left the water carrying a huge cleaver, his face a bleak mask. With one mighty blow he struck off his mother's head and watched it fall to the ground. Then, bending low, he picked up the head and carried it up the mountain. Here Isis was able to transform herself into a headless flint statue. The other gods watched, horror-struck and powerless to act. Horus had to be punished for his crime, but first he had to be caught. So the entire council, including Seth, went into the mountains in search of Horus, son, and now murderer, of Isis.

Horus was lying on his back in the shade of a tree, feeling the first stirrings of remorse, for he had truly loved his mother. Here Seth found him and attacked him. Seth was the stronger of the two, and he triumphed easily over his young adversary. Plucking out

Horus's eyes, he buried them in the ground. Then, abandoning his sightless nephew, Seth returned to the other gods and, without revealing that he had already fought Horus, helped them in their fruitless search. Meanwhile the two eyes became bulbs that grew into beautiful lotus blossoms on the mountainside.

Eventually, gentle Hathor found the blind Horus weeping from pain and self-pity in the barren desert. She knew exactly what to do. She caught a wild gazelle and milked it. Then she forced Horus to open his empty eyes so that she might cure them. Milk was dribbled into the left eye socket, and milk was dribbled into the right eye socket, and Horus was made whole again.

Once again the council summoned Horus and Seth. Weary of their quarrelling, the Universal Lord told the pair to try to resolve their differences amicably over a jug of wine, or perhaps a meal. And so Seth invited Horus to dine at his house that night. The two ate and drank until it grew dark, when a bed was prepared for them. Pleasantly drunk, they lay down together on the bed and fell asleep.

During the night Seth became aroused, and he slipped his erect penis between the sleeping Horus's legs. Horus, horrified, woke up and realised what was happening. He resisted, but could not stop his uncle. He caught Seth's semen in his hands and went crying to his mother. He told her what had happened, and showed her the semen still held in his fists. Isis let out a great shriek, and at once cut off Horus's contaminated hands and threw them into the water. By magic she fashioned her son a new pair of hands. Then she thought long and hard, for she suspected Seth of trickery rather than simple lust.

Fetching an exotic oil Isis massaged it into Horus's penis until it grew long and stiff. She used a pot to collect his semen. Then, early next morning, she visited Seth's garden and interviewed his head gardener. Learning that lettuce was Seth's favourite food, she sprinkled Horus's semen onto the lettuce patch. And when, later that day, Seth ate the lettuce in his garden he ate the semen too, and became pregnant with the seed of Horus.

Seth went to Horus and asked him to appear with him once again before the council of the gods. And here Seth condemned Horus before his fellow deities: "Let me be the King of Egypt, for Horus has allowed me to use him exactly as a man uses a woman".

The gods were horrified, and spat at Horus. But Horus merely laughed. Taking an oath, he spoke in turn. "All that Seth says is untrue: quite the opposite happened. Call forth our semen, and see whence it answers."

And so Thoth laid his hand on Horus's arm, and called to the semen of Seth. The semen answered not, as Seth had expected, from inside Horus, but from the depths of the waters. Then Thoth laid his hand on Seth's arm, and called to the semen of Horus. And it answered from inside Seth, and it emerged as the sun's disk on top of his head. Thoth took the golden disk from Seth's head and wore it as a crown. Seth was intensely angry, and very puzzled - he knew exactly what he had done - how could this have happened? On the basis of this evidence the gods gave their judgement.

"Horus is right and Seth is wrong."

Seth let out a great shriek, and issued a further, desperate challenge to Horus. They would both build boats of stone and race each other. Whoever won the race would wear the crown of Egypt. By now Horus had learned never to trust his uncle. He built a wooden boat which he covered in plaster and painted so that it looked like a ship carved from stone. Seth saw this ship and, believing it to be stone, built himself a stone boat. Of course, when the race started, Seth's stone boat sank while Horus's disguised wooden boat floated. Furious and frustrated, Seth transformed himself into a hippopotamus and holed Horus's boat. Horus seized a copper harpoon and attempted to spear Seth, until the council of the gods ordered that Seth should not be injured.

Horus sailed downriver to Sais, home of the Mother Goddess Neith. He intended to plead with her to intervene on his behalf, for he had been in dispute with his uncle for eighty years and, although he had been victorious in all the law courts in the land, he still did not have his throne. Realising this, the gods decided to write to Osiris and ask his advice. And so Thoth put paintbrush to papyrus, and a letter was duly dispatched to the Land of the Dead. As they might perhaps have expected Osiris was intensely displeased and replied by return. "Why is my only son being dispossessed, when you owe everything to me? I alone made you strong. I made barley and wheat to feed both the gods and mankind. No other god could have done this."

The Universal Lord was not impressed with this argument. He sent a cruelly accurate note back. "Barley and wheat would have existed even if you had never been born."

Osiris, stung to the core, sent a longer and more considered reply in defence of his son's claim. "You must give this matter your full attention, or something bad will surely happen to you. The land where I now dwell is full of daemons who fear none of you, neither god nor goddess. If I release these daemons they will rip out the heart of every wrongdoer, and bring it to me. The miscreants will then be forced to dwell here with me, forever. For I am the mightiest of us all. You, who are still blessed with life, have allowed injustice to come into being."

The gods listened to Osiris's scarcely veiled threat to release the daemons of the Underworld, and hastily declared Osiris to be right. Horus should inherit his father's throne. But Seth once again asked that he and Horus be taken to the Isle-in-the-Midst where they could compete for the crown. This was done, and Horus was once again victorious. Then, at last, the Universal Lord ordered Isis to bring Seth before him, bound in chains. And so, publicly humiliated, Seth was brought before his peers. Finally Seth agreed that Horus should be King of Egypt. Horus, son of Isis, was brought in triumph before his fellow gods. He was crowned with the White Crown, and placed on the throne of his father Osiris. Isis, happy at last, sang a hymn of triumph for her son.

As for Seth, he was not punished but sent to live with Re, where today he thunders in the sky bringing fear to the hearts of mankind.

COMMENTARY ON
THE DISPUTE OF HORUS AND SETH

The lengthy story of the conflict of Horus and Seth has survived on a single Theban papyrus dated to the 20th Dynasty reign of Ramesses V. But this papyrus retells a far more ancient story - the story of the struggles that eventually saw a long, narrow land of independent towns and city-states united under one king. Here Horus represents living Egyptian kingship while his father, Osiris, represents the long line of Egypt's dead kings and his uncle, Seth, represents the disorder that offers a constant threat to Egypt's unity. The struggle for the throne is not a straightforward contest fought fair and square. Each bout is won by trickery and cheating.

The gods whom we meet in this tale are not the awesome, omnipotent beings of our earlier encounters. The anonymous author intended his tale to be humorous rather than religious in tone, and so made his characters weak, gullible, indecisive and occasionally coarse and crude. As there are no humans in this tale, they are entirely responsible for their own mistakes and misfortunes.

The author lacked the ancient equivalent of a good editor, and to modern eyes his story is short on pace and action. But we should be careful here; the original audience, perhaps made up of professional scribes accustomed to the slow-moving wheels of Egyptian bureaucracy, may well have relished the constant repetition and the fruitless debates as an ironic comment on their own legal system. The divine council which attempts to decide who should rule Egypt certainly provides an excellent example of the worst sort of committee, capable of generating a great deal of hot air but incapable of reaching a firm decision. We know that the Egyptian civil courts often struggled to conclude a case and it seems that this at least is a true reflection of contemporary Egyptian life.

The Universal Lord, or All-Lord, leader of the council of the gods, is a combination of all the different manifestations of the sun god Re; he is Re-Atum-Horakhty-Khepri and probably a few others besides. At various points in the story the author uses a specific name for this being, so that he is sometimes referred to as Re, sometimes Atum. Here, to avoid confusion, I have referred to him as the Universal Lord throughout.

Horus the falcon, Lord of the Sky and hero of our tale, is one of Egypt's most ancient beings. We can see a form of Horus controlling a prisoner on the Predynastic Narmer Palette, while a falcon perches proudly on top of the *serekh* (a fore-runner of the cartouche) that encloses the names of the Archaic kings. Tradition tells us that Egypt's prehistoric princes were "Followers of Horus", and it seems highly probable that the influential Predynastic temple of Hierakonpolis, "City of the Hawk", was dedicated to a form of Horus. From earliest times Horus the hawk was both a sky god (his right eye the sun, his left eye the moon) and a sun god who in the more specialised form of Horakhty, "Horus of the Horizon", was specifically linked to the young, or rising, sun. Later, the story of Horus would be linked to the mythology of Isis and Osiris, allowing him to feature as the divine child.

Thoth appears in his dual role as scribe to the gods and friend to Osiris. In some earlier versions of this story Thoth is actually the son of Horus, who emerges from Seth's head after the latter's unwitting consumption of the polluted lettuce. Thoth was a lunar deity who, taking the form of either an ibis or a baboon, was strongly connected with writing and all forms of knowledge. Neith, the goddess whose opinion is held in such high regard by her fellow gods, is another long-established being. Celebrated as both a warrior and a creator, her title Mother of the Gods identifies her with the creative force present at the beginning of the world.

Banebdjedet of the Delta city of Mendes, in contrast, is an obscure deity of awesome sexual prowess, who takes the form of a ram and who is believed to represent the souls of Osiris, Re, Shu and Geb. The rude Babi is a baboon god, famed for his aggression and his sexual potency. He is a guardian of the sky and a friend of Seth. Anath and Astarte, mentioned as daughters of the Universal Lord and potential wives of Seth, are foreign warrior goddesses introduced to Egypt from the Near East; their inclusion in the story proves that this version, at least, does not predate the New Kingdom. Anath is a Syrian who makes her first Egyptian appearance during the Middle Kingdom, while the Western Semitic Astarte arrives during the New Kingdom. Both were welcomed into the pantheon, as tolerant Egypt was always willing to accept new deities.

In his struggle to claim his heritage Horus has right on his side. He is the son of the dead king and is clearly the heir to the Egyptian throne. And yet, for some inexplicable reason, he does not get full support from his fellow gods and the influential Universal Lord is very much on Seth's side. In this tale Seth certainly emerges as the more cunning and experienced political campaigner, and it is the impulsive Horus who commits by far the worst deeds.

The gods seem particularly appalled by the thought that Horus has enjoyed intercourse with his uncle: it is the homosexuality, or rather the implication that Horus has allowed himself to be emasculated, rather than the incest that shocks here. Homosexuality was by no means unknown in Egypt, but it did not fit with the idea of what was right and proper - the ideal family being a husband, a wife and as many children as possible. So our references to homosexuality come from popular culture rather than official sources. Homosexual rape was used as a means of degrading the unfortunate, and it was the victim rather than the aggressor who was deemed to have brought shame on himself. We should not be too certain that this is rape, real or attempted, however, as earlier versions of this same tale have Horus as an eager participant in their union.

Horus's attack on Isis, his widowed mother, is whatever way we look at it, a very bad thing. Respect for wives and mothers was a basic tenet of Egyptian family life, endorsed by scribes who urged their readers to care for their mothers just as they themselves had once been cared for, even under the most extreme and trying circumstances: "As you grew, and your excrement was disgusting, your mother was not disgusted". Fortunately, and we are not told how, Isis the healer, possessor of a magic strong enough to restore the dead to life, is able to re-attach her head to the flint statue and continue her spirited defence of her son's rights.

The ferryman, whose disobedience has caused all the trouble on the Isle-in-the-Midst, pays a high price for his shiny gold ring. In a fit of vindictiveness Seth demands that the ferryman be punished and his fellow gods agree. Amputation of the nose and or ears is a well-documented Egyptian punishment; the amputation of the toes, as in this story, is otherwise unknown.

In this version of the story Seth loses his claim to the throne, but is compensated with an honourable place in the solar boat of Re. In other versions of the tale he does not get off so lightly. At the Upper Egyptian city of Edfu, the annual Ptolemaic Festival of Victory included a re-enactment of the story of Horus and Seth. The drama ended with Seth, in the form of a hippopotamus, mortally pierced by ten harpoons. His body was subsequently dismembered and eaten, leaving no remains for burial.

SEVEN TALES OF MEN

There is little need to labour the importance of a nation's fiction as evidence of its national characteristics, its tastes and its customs; the thing is obvious, though not so much acknowledged as it might be.

James Baikie, *Egyptian Papyri and Papyrus Hunting*, 1925

5

FIVE MAGICAL TALES

THE FIRST STORY: THE MAGIC OCCURRING IN THE TIME OF KING DJOSER, TOLD BY AN UNKNOWN PRINCE

This story has been irretrievably damaged. All that we know is that its magic excited the admiration and respect of King Khufu.

THE SECOND STORY: THE MAGIC OCCURRING IN THE TIME OF KING NEBKA, TOLD BY PRINCE KHAEFRE

I would like to tell Your Majesty of another wonder. This miracle occurred during the rule of King Nebka, and it concerned the wise priest Webaoner. Webaoner was a respectable married man who owned a spacious villa with a green garden, shady fruit trees and a calm blue pool. He should have been the happiest man in Egypt. But his beautiful young wife had become infatuated with a handsome man she had glimpsed in the street. So obsessed was she, so filled with adulterous longings, that she dispatched a servant to the object of her desires, carrying as a present a chest filled with the most luxurious of garments. The man, overwhelmed with the generosity of the gift, returned with the servant to thank his benefactor in person. Having seen her beauty, he desired her greatly. The handsome man started to plan how he could sleep with the beautiful wife of Webaoner.

Several days passed by. Then the man sent a secret message to the wife of Webaoner.

"I know that there is a secluded gazebo in your garden, close by the pool. I also know that your husband spends many hours working away from home. Would it not be pleasant for you and I to spend some time together, relaxing in the gazebo? We could eat and drink together, and maybe even swim a little in the cool water."

The faithless wife needed little persuading - this was exactly what she had hoped for. She immediately summoned the household steward, and ordered that the gazebo be cleaned for the tryst, with food and drink prepared and fresh rushes strewn on the floor. And the next day saw the wife and her lover secluded in the gazebo, where they drank fine wine, ate choice foods, and lay together.

The loyal steward was troubled by what had happened, and reported the matter to his master. Outwardly calm, Webaoner was devastated by his wife's betrayal. He said nothing, but resolved to have his revenge. Sending for his precious chest, a beautiful wooden box inlaid with gold and ebony, he extracted a lump of wax and fashioned it into the form of a crocodile seven fingers long. As he worked he muttered secret, magical words over the small wax figure. Then he turned to his steward.

"Tomorrow, when the man goes down to the pool to bathe, throw this crocodile in after him."

The steward, frightened by what he had seen and heard, agreed at once to do as his master had said.

The next morning the wife again asked the steward to have the gazebo prepared for her guest. And she spent the remainder of the day luxuriating in the arms of her lover. But that evening, when the man went down to the pool to bathe, the steward threw the wax crocodile into the water after him. And the wax crocodile seven fingers long grew into a living beast seven cubits long, with cruel teeth, evil eyes and a thrashing tail. The crocodile seized the horrified lover in its powerful jaws and dragged him, shrieking and struggling, under the water.

Webaoner left home and worked for six days at the court of King Nebka. All this time his wife's lover remained under the water with the crocodile. On the seventh day Webaoner led King Nebka to his house, for he wished to have a witness to the curious events that were about to unfold in his garden. Standing on the edge of the calm blue pool, Webaoner called his creation forth. And the water bubbled and foamed and surged, and out of the depths the enormous crocodile emerged, with the unhappy lover still twitching in its jaws. Webaoner called on the crocodile to release its victim, and the crocodile placed the shivering man on the grassy bank next to the king, who drew back in alarm. Then Webaoner bent down and, totally fearless, picked up the crocodile. Instantly it turned back to wax in his hands.

Webaoner told King Nebka the full story of his faithless wife and her handsome lover. The king paused for a moment's thought, then issued stern judgement. The crocodile was to take what belonged to him; at once the wax figure came back to life and, picking up the man, slithered into the water, never to be seen again. As for the wife, she was to be taken from the house and burned, and her ashes scattered over the pool that had become her lover's grave. And this is the marvel that happened in the time of Nebka.

THE THIRD STORY: THE MAGIC OCCURRING IN THE TIME OF KING SNEFRU, TOLD BY PRINCE BAUEFRE

Now I will tell Your Majesty of yet another wonderful event, one that happened at the court of your esteemed late father, Snefru. As you well know, King Snefru was the richest and most blessed man in the whole world. He had everything that anyone could wish for - great heaps of gold, granaries overflowing with corn and warehouses filled with wine. He had a fleet of wooden ships, three magnificent pyramids and a harem full of beautiful women. But inside his magnificent palace he had grown bored and discontent as only the very rich can be. He wandered from room to room seeking something, anything, which would entertain him for an hour. Finally he summoned the High Priest Djadja-em-Ankh, and sought his advice. Djadja-em-Ankh did not fail his king - he proposed a wonderful plan.

Snefru made his way to the palace lake. Here a throne had been prepared for him, carefully positioned so that he could admire Egypt in all her glory; the sparkling blue water and the clear blue sky, the sandy shore and the fertile green fields and mountains beyond. But Snefru was not interested in studying the beauties of nature. His attention was firmly fixed on the lake. Here twenty of Egypt's most beautiful maidens - virgins, each blessed with a curvaceous body, firm breasts and elaborately braided hair - were rowing up and down using oars made from ebony and gold. Best of all, and this was the king's own idea, the maidens wore nothing but simple shift dresses made out of fishermen's nets.

Out on the sunlit water the maidens rowed with a slow, steady stroke. They sang as they rowed, their golden skin glistening with sweat, their braids swinging in rhythm with their song, and their net dresses tracing exciting patterns on their bare flesh. Never had Snefru been so happy. But suddenly the tranquillity of the moment was broken. The leading maiden cried out in distress. A precious fish-shaped charm had fallen from her hair and was lost in the water. The rowers laid down their oars in confusion; the boats stopped moving and the happy voices faded away. The king quickly promised to replace the turquoise charm - he would have promised anything to start the girls rowing again - but the maiden could not be comforted. She wanted her own lucky charm, not a new one, and she wanted it now. It seemed that the happy spectacle was over.

Again Snefru sent for Djadja-em-Ankh. He explained the situation, and asked for help. The High Priest did not hesitate. He spoke just one magical word and the waters of the lake became solid. Carefully folding one side of the lake back onto the other, Djadja-em-Ankh reached down and collected the charm which he found lying on a piece of broken pot on the exposed lake bed. A second command restored the lake to its watery form, and the maidens took to their boats again.

Snefru was mightily impressed by what he had seen. The High Priest's triumph was celebrated that evening with a great feast lasting well into the night. And Djadja-em-Ankh was rewarded with many valuable gifts.

THE FOURTH STORY: THE MAGIC OCCURRING IN THE TIME OF KING KHUFU, TOLD BY PRINCE HARDJEDEF

Prince Hardjedef spoke. "You have just listened to three tales of powerful magic performed by great men who are now dead and living with Osiris in the Underworld. But who can tell if these wonderful events truly happened? Yet there is a man living today, one of Your Majesty's own subjects, who is truly a superb magician. A man named Djedi lives in the town of Djed-Snefru. He is a man already 110 years old, yet he eats five hundred loaves of bread and half a cow every day, and he washes his meal down with at least one hundred jugs of beer. And this man can rejoin a severed head. He can tame a lion so that it walks behind him like a cat, its lead trailing on the ground. And he knows the number and plan of the secret chambers in the Sanctuary of Thoth."

King Khufu was greatly intrigued by his son's words. For he had long been fascinated by the riddle of the chambers of Thoth, and had spent many years researching their secret in the hope that he might be able to recreate them in his own pyramid complex. He ordered Prince Hardjedef to bring the magician to him at once.

Hardjedef had a fleet of boats prepared, then sailed upriver in splendid style to Djed-Snefru. When the fleet had moored he disembarked to travel overland, seated in a carrying chair carved of ebony, whose poles were decorated with gold. And so the son of Khufu reached the house of Djedi the magician.

Prince Hardjedef clambered out of his carrying chair. He found the wise old man lying on a mat in the courtyard of his house. One servant squatted beside his master, massaging his bald scalp with scented oils; a second servant squatted to rub his master's hard and horny feet. Hardjedef was amazed. For Djedi was a man so old that death must surely be looming near, yet he had all the vigour and health of a young man with no sign of senility, not even a cough, to betray his true age.

The prince hailed the old man courteously.

"Greetings, O great sage. I have come to welcome you to the court of my father, King Khufu. There you may eat the finest of foods, and drink the best of wines. And when the time comes, my father will ensure that you have an honourable funeral with burial in the cemetery of your forefathers."

The old man addressed the prince with equal respect.

"Welcome in peace Hardjedef, beloved son of Khufu. May your father shower you with praise. May he promote you above all your brothers. May your spirit triumph over all your enemies, and may your soul lead you safely, at the right time, to the dark doorway that allows entry to the eternal life."

Then the prince held out his hands and pulled the old man gently to his feet. Linking arms they walked together to the mooring place of Djed-Snefru. Here Djedi stopped.

"Allow me the luxury of a boat to carry my household and my precious library to the palace."

Hardjedef allocated the magician two barges and their crews for the transportation of his goods and chattels, but he insisted that his honoured guest should sail in the greater comfort of his own royal boat. And thus Djedi the magician sailed downstream to the court of King Khufu.

King Khufu could hardly wait to see the magician of whom so much had been told. Rushing to the great pillared hall of the palace, quite forgetting his manners in his eagerness, he fired a question at the old man.

"How can it be that I have never seen you before, Djedi?"

With great wisdom, the old man replied.

"Only he that is summoned can respond, my king. You have now summoned me, and I have come at once. How can I help you?"

"Is it true what they say, that you can rejoin a severed head?"

"Yes, my king, I can."

In great excitement Khufu ordered that a prisoner be brought from the gaol, so that he might be beheaded and restored to life. But Djedi halted him.

"Surely there is no need to execute anyone, my king. For murder is forbidden by our law. Let us kill an animal instead."

And so a goose was brought into the great pillared hall, and its head was cut off as everyone watched. Its body was placed on the west side of the hall, and its head was placed on the east. Djedi uttered his magical spell. And at once the body of the goose stood up and waddled towards its head, while the head started to jerk and roll towards its body. The two halves of the bird met in the middle of the chamber and were joined, so that the goose was whole and live and cackling again.

Khufu watched, open mouthed, as Djedi repeated his trick first with a long-legged ibis and then, most impressively, with a full-grown bull. Finally, as an encore, a roaring lion was dragged in, and the magician demonstrated that he could indeed tame the savage beast with just one word, so that it walked behind him, gentle as a kitten. Djedi had proved himself, and Khufu now posed the question that had obsessed him for many years.

"They tell me that you know the number and plan of the hidden chambers in the Sanctuary of Thoth. Will you now reveal this secret to me?"

But Djedi shook his head. "I do not know the secret, my king, but I do know where it may be read. There is a chest carved from flint in the building known as the Inventory in the city of Heliopolis. But I cannot bring this to you. Only the eldest of the three unborn sons in the womb of the Lady Redjedet can bring this chest to you."

The king's face fell. For he greatly desired to open the chest and discover its contents.

"But who is this Lady Redjedet? I have never heard of her."

"She is the wife of a priest of Re, Lord of Sakhbu, my king. She is destined to give birth to the three mortal sons of Re. They will hold the highest office in the land, and the eldest son will become High Priest of Re."

On hearing this prophesy Khufu's heart grew sad, for he had assumed that his own sons and grandsons and their sons and grandsons in turn would occupy the throne of Egypt until the end of time. Djedi noticed his king's abrupt change of mood.

"Why this sorrow, my king? Is it because I have told you about the three kings who are to come? Don't worry - first your son will rule, then his son, and only then will one of the three take his place."

Slightly consoled, the king asked: "When will the Lady Redjedet give birth?"

"She will go into labour on the fifteenth day of the first month of winter", the magician replied.

"Oh no. The sandbanks of the Two Fishes Canal will be dry at that time. Otherwise I could perhaps have gone to see this wonderful thing with my own eyes, and visited the magnificent temple of Re, Lord of Sakhbu, at the same time."

"Do not worry, my king. When the time comes I will make sure that there is water four cubits deep on the sandbanks of the Two Fishes Canal. You will be able to cross over whenever you desire."

Djedi had proved to be everything that Hardjedef had claimed for him, and more. Khufu commanded that the magician should dwell for the rest of his life as an honoured guest amongst Hardjedef's household. His rations were to be set at one thousand loaves of bread, one hundred jugs of beer, one ox and one hundred bundles of green vegetables. And as the king had commanded, so it was done.

THE FIFTH STORY: THE MAGIC OCCURRING
IN THE FUTURE

The day came when Redjedet, wife of the priest Rewoser, felt the first sharp pangs of childbirth and took to her bedchamber. There she stayed for many hours, for her labour was long and very painful, and it seemed that nothing could be done to help her. The great god Re, seeing her plight, summoned Isis, Nephthys, Meskhenet and Heket to him. Re begged the four goddesses to assist Redjedet, and to ensure that her three children were safely delivered. For the three unborn children were the three sons of Re, destined to rule Egypt as kings. Eventually, as Re foretold, they would build shrines and make magnificent offerings to the goddesses who had helped at their birth. Pausing only to disguise themselves as dancing girls, the goddesses departed for Egypt, and with them went the great creator god Khnum, dressed as a servant and carrying the birthing stool.

Rewoser was standing outside his house, his kilt disordered and his mind preoccupied with thoughts of his wife's suffering. The goddesses showed him their rattles and their necklaces, and he asked at once for their help.

"For my wife is in much pain, and her labour is very difficult. I am afraid that she and her unborn child might die."

The goddesses entered the house and went straight to Redjedet, locking the door of her room behind them so that no one could enter and see their deeds.

The time for delivery had come. Redjedet squatted to give birth. Isis stood in front of her, Nephthys stood behind her, and Heket performed the magic that would hasten the delivery. Isis greeted the first child:

"Do not be so strong in your mother's womb, you whose name means Strong."

And a baby boy slipped into her arms; a sturdy child, one cubit long, with golden flesh and a head-dress of real lapis lazuli. The baby was washed, his umbilical cord was severed, and he was placed on a cushion. Meskhenet confirmed his fate:

"A king who will rule over the entire land".

Then Khnum, the creator god, gave him the gift of health.

Again the goddesses took up their positions. Isis stood in front of Redjedet, Nephthys stood behind her, and Heket performed the magic that would hasten the birth. Isis spoke to the baby:

"Do not kick in your mother's womb, you whose name means Kicker".

And a second baby slid out into her arms; another sturdy son, one cubit long, with golden flesh and a head-dress of real lapis lazuli. This baby, too, was washed, his cord was cut and he was placed on a cushion. Meskhenet confirmed his fate:

"A king who will rule over the entire land".

And Khnum, the creator god, gave him the gift of health.

For the third time the goddesses moved to help the young mother. Isis stood in front of her, Nephthys behind, and Heket performed her magic. Isis spoke again:

"Do not be dark in your mother's womb, you whose name means Dark".

And the third baby dropped into her arms; again a sturdy boy, one cubit long, with golden flesh and a head-dress of real lapis lazuli. Meskhenet confirmed his fate:

"A king who will rule over the entire land".

Once again Khnum, the creator god, gave the gift of health.

Then the baby was washed, his cord was cut and he was placed on a cushion beside his brothers.

The three goddesses left the new mother to rest with her children, and went in search of the new father, whom they had barred from the delivery room. Quickly, they broke the good news to him.

"Give thanks to the gods, Rewoser, for your wife has given birth to three fine sons, and all four are healthy and well."

Rewoser was overjoyed, and filled with gratitude. At once he offered the dancing girls his only sack of barley in payment for their labours for, as he said, this was a most valuable and useful gift that they could use to make bread and beer. The goddesses accepted the payment gladly, and gave it to Khnum to carry, for it was heavy.

They set off from the house, but had only travelled a little way along the road before Isis had second thoughts.

"Why are we going straight home? We have not yet performed a marvel for these three precious children."

So they made three royal crowns, and hid them in the sack of barley. And then, having conjured up a fierce storm, they returned to shelter at the house of the priest. They asked Rewoser to store the sack for them: "For we are going north to dance, and do not want to be burdened with a heavy sack".

Rewoser did as they asked, and the sack was locked in an unused room.

Redjedet rested in bed for fourteen days, and then prepared to leave her chamber and resume her household duties. She asked her maidservant, "Is everything in the house made ready for me?"

"Everything is prepared, my lady, except for the beer - we don't have any jars of beer."

"Why don't we have any jars of beer?" Redjedet snapped, irritated with her careless maid.

"Because we have no grain in the house to make beer, except for one sack of barley which now belongs to the four dancing girls and their servant."

After a moment's pause Redjedet told the maidservant to open up the sack and take some of the barley, for she knew that her husband was an honourable man who would replace anything that she had borrowed when the musicians returned from the north.

The servant took a basket and unlocked the door of the chamber that held the barley. Briskly she entered the room, then stood stock still in amazement. For she could hear music and singing and all kinds of good sounds in the empty room, but she could not tell where they came from. Turning on her heels, she fled in fear to her mistress. Next Redjedet entered the room, sceptical but urged on by her maidservant. She too could hear the noise of celebrations, but could not tell whence it came until she put her ear against the sack of barley. And then she knew, and she understood that something wonderful was happening in her house. Her heart was filled with a great joy.

Redjedet ordered that the sack be locked in a box which was itself sealed in a larger chest and bound with a leather strap. Finally the chest was locked in the secure room that contained her own most precious belongings. That night, when Rewoser returned from work, she told him what had happened and he too was filled with great happiness and wonder. And they celebrated, long into the night, with a magnificent banquet.

With the sack secure against prying eyes and the maidservant sworn to secrecy, life slowly returned to normal in the house of the priest of Re. Until, many days later, Redjedet had reason to find fault with her careless maid, and punished her with a well-deserved beating. The maidservant was incensed, and her secret knowledge burned within her.

"Who is she to treat me this way? She has given birth to three future kings, but is keeping them a secret. This is treason. I will go to the city and tell King Khufu exactly what is being plotted in the house of Rewoser."

Running from the house the maidservant set off for the palace. Her path took her past the farm where she found her half-brother binding bundles of flax. Surprised to see his little sister flushed with running, he asked where she was going in such haste. She told him all that she had seen and heard in the house of Rewoser, and of her determination to betray the three babies to the current king. Her brother, both older and wiser than she, immediately realised that his heedless little sister should be stopped. He certainly did not want to be involved in her dangerous gossip. He lashed out at her with his bundle of flax. Then he sent her off to the canal to fill a jug with water so that they might both have a drink and talk the matter over sensibly. But while the maid was by the canal filling her jug, a crocodile rose out of the water and dragged her under. She was never seen again.

With a heavy heart the brother made his way to the house of Rewoser, to report what had happened to his sister. And there he found the Lady Redjedet hunched in her chair, weeping.

"My lady, why are you so upset?"

"I am upset because I am thinking of the little girl who grew up in this house, whom I loved almost as a daughter, and who became my maid. Just now she was naughty and I had to punish her. She took great offence, and ran off to tell the king the amazing things that have happened here. She intends to betray my babies, and I don't know how to stop her."

Hearing these sad words the brother's heart was moved. He hastened to reassure Redjedet. "Do not worry, my lady. My foolish sister did indeed start to tell me about the wonderful things that have happened under your roof. But I would not listen. I hit her to stop her talking, then I sent her to draw water so that we might have a drink and talk things over, calmly. And while she was by the water a crocodile took her. She is dead, and will talk no more. Your secret, and your sons, are safe..."

COMMENTARY ON
FIVE MAGICAL TALES

Here we have five independent fictional tales, linked together as a series of stories about kings past and present. They are told by the royal princes, who have set out to entertain their father, the real 4th Dynasty King Khufu. Today they are preserved as twelve columns of text on a single, damaged, manuscript of uncertain provenance known as Papyrus Westcar (Berlin Museum). This document was written during the Second Intermediate Period of Hyksos rule, but the stories themselves appear to be Middle Kingdom in origin.

Khufu (Cheops to the Greeks) has been given a bad press by the classical writers, who regarded him as a cruel tyrant loathed by his family and his people alike. Their histories tell of a reign of blasphemy, closed temples and exploited slaves, and the Greek historian Herodotus adds a sordid tale of an abused daughter to complete the picture. These damning character assessments are based on the assumption that Egypt must have suffered - and suffered most horribly - to build Khufu's Great Pyramid. The classical writers, of course, lived many centuries after Khufu and knew nothing about the economics of pyramid building. We, with the advantage of modern archaeology, know that they were wrong. Khufu did not have access to thousands of slaves, and his pyramid was built by skilled craftsmen who were well fed, well housed and treated with a great deal of respect. As to the king's character, we really do not have enough evidence to make sensible comment. His reign, apart from his pyramid building, is an obscure one, and our only image of the once mighty king is a small ivory carving, three inches high. However, in these tales at least, Khufu appears as a sane and rational being. His only flaw is his understandable eagerness to execute a human prisoner, and this may perhaps be excused as Khufu believes that the prisoner will be instantly restored to life.

Unfortunately the first story is almost entirely lost, although we do know that it was set in the time of Djoser, first king of the 3rd Dynasty. It may well have involved magic performed by the real-life priest and vizier Imhotep. Imhotep, "Overseer of Works" for King Djoser, was credited with designing and building the Sakkara Step Pyramid, Egypt's first stone building. After his death he was deified, and worshipped as a god of medicine and learning.

The second story visits the 3rd Dynasty court of King Nebka. It is told by Prince Khaefre (Chephren), who is destined to rule Egypt as the fourth king of the 4th Dynasty, and who will build the second of the Giza pyramids and the Great Sphinx. It is a tale of desire, betrayal and revenge; the faithless wife tempts the innocent man, and both must pay the price for their lust. This is an often-repeated theme of Egyptian literature, and the great didactic texts - instructions written to tell young men how to behave - are full of warnings against approaching married women. As the Old Kingdom sage Ptah-Hotep wisely remarked:

> *If you want friendships to last in the house that you enter as a master, brother or friend, wherever you enter, beware of approaching the women!*

However, the interest of this tale is not in the adultery, which is somewhat commonplace, but in the magic performed by the wise husband. Webaoner has a very powerful magic - he can control the crocodile, the untameable destroyer that lurks on Egypt's river-banks, and he can ensure that a man remains alive after seven days under water. Wronged though he has been, Webaoner is careful not to take the law into his own hands. Adultery is not a capital offence, and it is only when he has the approval of the king - Egypt's ulti-mate judge - that he allows his crocodile to kill its prey. His choice of animal is a deliberate one. The Egyptians often used the croco-dile to symbolise destiny or fate and it is no coincidence that the garrulous serving girl in our fifth magical tale is also taken by a crocodile. Webaoner's is a large, but not unfeasibly large, beast. A cubit measured just over 20.5 inches (52.5 cm), and so the croco-dile must have been 12 ft (3.6 metres) long. Webaoner's unfaithful wife meets an equally unpleasant end. It is not made clear whether she is to be burned alive or cremated after death, but either way she would leave no body for burial, and so would be effectively barred from the Afterlife.

The third story is set at the relatively recent court of the kindly King Snefru, father of Khufu and builder of the one Meidum and two of the Dahshur pyramids. It is told by Bauefre, a prince who has left no known tomb but whose name is recorded on a list of royal names carved during the Middle Kingdom in the Wadi Hammamat. He might perhaps be the "Prince Babaef" who was buried in the Giza cemetery. Snefru is infinitely rich, and infinitely bored - boredom being a privilege of the elite in hard-working Egypt. Snefru seems to have been particularly prone to attacks of ennui, and the Middle Kingdom *Prophecies of Neferti* tells of a sepa-rate occasion when the bored king sent for a sage famed for his entertaining oratory. Incurious about his country's past, Snefru chose to enjoy a glimpse into his country's future. Whether or not Neferti was disconcerted by the fact that his king wrote down every word he uttered we cannot tell.

Snefru's tale, like Nebka's tale, is centred on a pool. But this is an innocuous confection of hot weather, cool water, pretty girls, mild voyeurism and, of course, spectacular magic. There is no life-threatening crocodile here. The scanty garments that the girls wear - designed by Snefru himself - are usually translated as fish-net dresses. They are more likely to be the beaded over-tunics that wealthy women wore over plain white sheaths on more formal occasions. The turquoise fish-shaped ornament that falls out of the maiden's hair may well have been a charm against drowning. If so, we can understand her reluctance to continue rowing without it.

The fourth tale brings the listeners up to date, for it is set in the time of Khufu himself. Prince Hardjedef never ruled Egypt, but he was obviously a person of great importance, who was accorded the honour of a large tomb in the royal cemetery near his father's pyramid. In death he was celebrated as a sage, and *The Instructions of Hardjedef*, a didactic text written by an anonymous scribe during the 5th Dynasty, was well respected as a guide to dynastic life. Unlike his brothers, Hardjedef does not actually tell a story. Instead he asks permission to bring a living magician to the court. Djedi the magician lives at Djed-Snefru, the town associated with the late King Snefru's pyramid complex. His magic is the most impressive yet, and he too can tame untameable beasts and move water. But Khufu is only really interested in the plan of the secret chambers of Thoth - a theme that is introduced to the story and then tantalisingly dropped. This casual mention of lost chambers has led to much speculation, and many published words, as both conventional and alternative Egyptologists attempt to understand its meaning.

The fifth story naturally follows on from the fourth. We are now in the future, and three 5th Dynasty kings of Egypt are about to be born - Userkaf, Sahure and Neferirkare. It is understandable that this story worries Khufu, who had hoped that his bloodline would stretch forever. Djedi attempts to reassure his king by confirming that his son (Khaefre) and his grandson (Menkaure; builder of the third Giza pyramid) will rule Egypt: in fact Khufu would be succeeded by his son Djedefre, and Menkaure would be followed by Shepseskaf, whose death saw the end of the 4th Dynasty. In any case, Userkaf, a king of mysterious origins, may well have been a descendent of Djedefre or Menkaure, so this may not have been the end of Khufu's line.

The 5th Dynasty kings were dedicated to the sun god Re. Here the three children incorporate Re's name within their own, and each will eventually build both a pyramid and a sun temple dedicated to his "father". The Lady Redjedet is likely to be a distorted, fictionalised version of the queen regnant Khentkawes I, mother of the first two kings of the 5th Dynasty.

Stories of miraculous royal births are not uncommon, and are certainly not confined to Ancient Egypt. Several of Egypt's kings would claim semi-divine origins, with the New Kingdom monarchs Hatshepsut, Amenhotep III and Ramesses II being perhaps the best-known and most successful children of gods. This story is unusual, however, in that it concentrates on the birth while leaving the conception to the imagination; in so doing, it offers our most complete glimpse into the secrets of Egyptian childbirth. This was always a difficult time; a time when the uncontrollable forces of creation and death came uncomfortably close to the living, and so it was a time where female magic rather than male medicine dominated. Women relied on the services of family members and midwives to get them through their ordeal. Here Re selects Isis, Nephthys, Heket and Meskhenet to help the stricken mother. We have already met Isis and Nephthys who, although strongly associated with death and mourning rituals, are also regarded as agents of healing and rebirth. Heket is a frog-headed goddess who carries the gift of life, while Meskhenet is a goddess of childbirth who decides the destiny of the new born. Although the goddesses are disguised as dancing girls, Rewoser has little difficulty in recognising them as itinerant midwives and he is happy to employ them to help his wife.

Rewoser is barred from the birth chamber, although the male god Khnum is allowed admittance. The enigmatic words uttered by Isis as the babies are born are plays on their names that the Egyptian readers would have recognised. "Do not be so strong in your mother's womb, you whose name means Strong" identifies

Userkaf, first king of the 5th Dynasty, whose name translates as "his Ka (spirit) is Strong". "Do not kick in your mother's womb, you whose name means Kicker" refers to the second king of the 5th Dynasty Sahure, a name which means "well-endowed by Re" but which includes the element *sahu*, "to kick". "Do not be dark in your mother's womb, you whose name means Dark" is spoken to Neferirkare Kakai, third king of the dynasty. The element *keku* in his name implies darkness.

The story has an abrupt ending, as the final part of the papyrus is missing. But it seems that the story was nearing its finish anyway, and we may not have lost too much of the narrative.

6

THE SHIPWRECKED SAILOR

The great ship had at last reached its port. The sails were furled, the gangplank had been lowered, and the sailors were hurrying ashore in high good humour, eager to spend their wages. Their long voyage had made them hungry for beer, for fresh bread and meat and, of course, for women. But not everyone was happy, and not everyone was rushing to disembark. Huddled in his cabin, the High Official sat silent and unmoving on his stool. He had failed in his mission, and was now very frightened indeed. How would the king react to his failure? What would be his fate?

A royal attendant approached the High Official, speaking with all the familiarity of a favoured servant.

"Cheer up, my lord. We have reached home safely, and our boat is now secure in its mooring. You should be thanking the gods for our good luck. We have survived a long and difficult journey, and have travelled all the way from Nubia without any loss of life amongst the crew. And that is a very good thing indeed.

"Now listen to me. You must pull yourself together, and snap out of your depression. Have a wash and a shave, put on clean clothes, and make yourself look decent. Prepare yourself to face the king and be ready to answer when questioned. You will be able to explain to him exactly what happened without hesitating over your words, and your speech will save you."

The High Official, brooding over his shattered career, made no move. And the attendant, irritated by his silence, lost all patience with him.

"Do as you like then, it is up to you. Give in, and do nothing to save yourself. It is a waste of time talking to you. But remember, disaster can turn to unexpected triumph. Something similar happened to me once. Listen, while I tell you my story:

"A long time ago I too went to the land of mines in the service of my king. I sailed on the great green sea in a massive ship, one hundred and twenty cubits long and forty cubits wide, crewed by a hundred and twenty of Egypt's most experienced sailors. A fine, lion-hearted bunch they were, the bravest and the best in the whole land. They could predict a storm before it broke, and see a torrent of rain before it happened.

"For many days our voyage went well and we made good time with a strong wind behind us. Then, with little warning, a violent storm broke while we were in the middle of the great green sea, far away from land. The heavens grew dark and angry, and the sea threw up huge foam-flecked waves, each larger than the last. Our boat rocked dangerously, and there was nothing we could do. We clung to the ropes in fear until one enormous wave, it must have been at least eight cubits high, smashed down on us, snapping the mast and bringing it thundering down on the deck. That was the end. The ship sank, and the rest of the crew were drowned. I was the only survivor. The waves carried me to a sandy shore and I crawled up the beach to the shelter of a grove of trees. And there I lay semi-conscious for three days and three nights.

"On the fourth day, slowly regaining my senses and my strength, I staggered to my feet and looked around for something to eat, for I was famished. I was very lucky. I discovered that I was on an island stocked with the most tempting of foods. I found figs and grapes, and all kinds of fine vegetables including cucumbers as tasty as those picked from the best gardens. There were plump fish swimming in the sea, and fat fowl sitting in the trees. There was nothing that I wanted to eat that I could not find. I ate and ate until

I was stuffed full and could eat no more. Then I cut myself a fire drill, lit a fire, and made a burnt offering to the gods who had saved me.

"Then I heard it. A low rumbling, thundering noise. The earth shook, the trees splintered, and I fell to the ground, squeezing my eyes shut and hiding my face in fear. I thought that another enormous wave was about to carry me out to sea, and I clung to the ground in panic.

"When I plucked up the courage to open my eyes I found that I was facing something far worse than a mere wave. A gigantic golden snake was slithering towards me, his head raised up, as if about to strike. This was no ordinary snake. He was at least thirty cubits in length. His eyebrows were formed from precious blue lapis lazuli and his beard was long and impressive.

"The snake noticed me cowering on the ground, and hissed:

'Who brought you here, sailor? If you do not tell me at once, I will destroy you utterly.'

"Trembling with fear I tried to make a sensible reply, but could only stutter. The snake listened in silence, then lowered his magnificent head and picked me up in his mouth. He carried me to his den, and placed me gently on the ground. Then he hissed at me again, this time with greater kindness.

'Who brought you here, sailor, to my island in the great green sea?'

"And I answered him with a rush of words, telling him all about the magnificent ship, the terrible storm, the enormous wave and the death of my companions.

"He spoke again to me, hissing softly:

'Do not be afraid, sailor. Do not tremble with fear now that you have come to me. The gods have decided that you should live, and have brought you to this ghost island. It is an island that lacks for nothing that a man might desire. It is an island full of good things. You shall live here for four months. Then a ship will come from Egypt, crewed by your friends. You will go home with them and will eventually die after a long life in your home town.'

"Then the snake grew thoughtful and sad, and a crystal tear fell from his eye.

'How happy is the man who is able to tell of his adventures long after his suffering has ended. I have a similar story of disaster to tell, but my story can have no happy ending. Many years ago I lived on this blessed island with my wife and my brothers and their wives and children. All together we were seventy-five giant snakes plus my much-loved little daughter, who had been granted to me by the gods after many years of longing and prayer. We were one happy family, and life was good. But one day, while I was away hunting for food, a flaming star fell from the sky. It burned up our village, and when I returned to my home everyone had died. I myself wished to die when I saw the charred heap of corpses, but I was destined to live on, alone. And I tell you this. If you are brave, and strong in heart, you will see your home and hug your children and kiss your wife once again.'

"Quaking on the ground before the magnificent snake I felt a wave of gratitude wash over me. I was not going to be eaten - I would see my home and family again. Impulsively, I spoke without thinking.

'I will tell the King of Egypt of your kindness to me. I will send you precious oils, and fragrant perfumes, and ships full of treasure. Everyone in the world shall hear of your goodness. I will slaughter geese and oxen for you as a burnt offering. For this is how we treat the gods who befriend lost Egyptians far away from home.'

"At this the snake hissed and spat with laughter, for my words must have seemed foolish to one so great.

'Don't be silly. I know that you are a poor sailor who could never afford such splendid gifts. Besides, I am the Lord of Punt, and I have all the oils and precious perfumes that I need right here on my island. Just make sure that my deeds are known in your land - that will be reward enough for me. Now must I tell you this. This island will vanish when you leave it, and turn to water and waves and dissolve into the great sea. Once you have gone from me, you can never come back.'

"And everything happened exactly as the giant snake had predicted. The ship came, crewed by people from my village. I sighted it from the top of a tall tree and went to tell the snake what I had seen. Of course, he already knew. I made my farewell, bowing low, and the snake gave me precious gifts; perfumes, oils, eye-paint, giraffe tails, huge lumps of incense, elephant tusks, long-tailed monkeys and much, much more. I loaded these presents onto the ship, and we sailed north, to Egypt. Two months later we reached the royal palace. I disembarked, and I presented my goods to the king. He rewarded me by making me a royal attendant with servants of my own. And this is how my disaster was turned into triumph."

As he finished his long story the attendant looked encouragingly at the High Official. But the Official was not brave enough to face up to his problems and make the best of a bad situation. He spoke for the first time, with great bitterness:

"Do not try to help me, my friend. My doom is come, and who would give water to a goose that is about to be slaughtered?"

He refused to leave the ship and continued to sit huddled on his chair, quaking with fear.

COMMENTARY ON
THE SHIPWRECKED SAILOR

This Middle Kingdom story is preserved on a single papyrus (Papyrus Leningrad 1115) now housed in the Hermitage Museum, St Petersburg. It is substantially complete and the papyrus shows no sign of damage, although the somewhat abrupt beginning has led to speculation that the scribe may have missed something out. A coda tells us that this scribe was Amen-aa, son of Ameny.

It is a fantastic and somewhat complex tale told mainly in the first person, with a story (told by the anonymous snake) within a story (told by the anonymous sailor) within a story. As we move deeper into these stories, we enter increasingly unreal worlds. Experts have long debated the true meaning of this tale; accepted interpretations range from the simple folk or fairy-tale, through a fictionalised account of the sun's daily voyage across the sky, or a coded manual for living the ideal life, to a complicated allegory dealing with mankind's lonely journey through the cosmos to stand before a nameless creator god who takes the form of a snake. Perhaps it contains elements of all of these, plus more that we cannot today identify.

The choice of a snake as the main force for good is perhaps puzzling to modern readers who tend to see snakes as unambiguous agents of evil. The Egyptians had a less clear-cut attitude. They rightly feared snakes as they feared any dangerous animal, but they also respected them - a snake in the granary was no bad thing, as it would eat the rats and mice and so protect the stored grain. This explains why there are both good and bad snake deities. On the bad side we have Apophis, the gigantic serpent who launches a nightly assault on the solar boat of Re. On the good side we have Mehen, the coiled snake who protects Re even as Apophis attacks. The snake goddess Meretseger guarded the Theban necropolis including the Valley of the Kings, while the ever-popular goddess of the harvest, Renenutet, protected granaries, houses and families, paying particular attention to the welfare of babies. Wadjet, the snake deity of Lower Egypt and the Nile Delta, is perhaps the best known of the benign snake deities. She appears in the uraeus, the cobra and vulture device that decorates and protects the royal crown.

The snake tells the sailor that his island will sink beneath the waves once the sailor has sailed away. In this way, the island becomes the reverse of the mound that we saw emerging from the sea of chaos in *The Creation of the World*. The location of this extraordinary Brigadoon-like disappearing island is, not surprisingly, hard for us to pinpoint although we are helped in our quest by the snake's title, "Lord of Punt". Punt was a real, far distant and now vanished trading post lying somewhere along the Eritrean/Ethiopian coast. Travel to Punt meant first dragging or carrying a flat-packed ship overland to the coast, then a lengthy voyage on the dangerous, unfamiliar sea. Good river sailors though they were, the Egyptians were never very confident on open water, so a successful expedition to Punt soon became the unmistakable hallmark of a divinely inspired reign. Visits to Punt were a feature of several Middle Kingdom reigns, and Montuhotep III, Senwosret I and Amenemhat II each sent expeditions. But the most famous expedition of all was that conducted by the female pharaoh Hatshepsut several centuries after our story was written. So impressed was Hatshepsut with her achievement, and its vindication of her atypical reign, that she recorded the voyage in a series of cartoons and brief texts on the wall of her mortuary temple at Deir el-Bahari. Expeditions continued during the reigns of Tuthmosis III and Amenhotep III but petered out during the 20th Dynasty, so that by the end of the Dynastic age Punt had become an unreal land, the stuff of myths and legends.

Hatshepsut's drawings, propaganda though they undoubtedly

are, allow us some understanding of the journey undertaken by our anonymous sailor. Five Egyptian sailing ships arrive at Punt and the sailors disembark into small boats and make for the shore. Here they find a village set in an exotic and totally un-Egyptian looking forest of ebony, incense and palm trees, its houses resembling large beehives set on poles so that their only means of access is by ladder. The Egyptian envoy Neshi is greeted by the friendly chief of Punt and his queen. The slender chief has a long thin goatee beard and a series of bracelets on his left leg. His wife is grotesquely fat, and presents a deliberately amusing contrast to the stereotyped image of upper class Egyptian beauty. The Egyptians present the Puntites with a small heap of trinkets, and invite them to a meal in their camp. When next we see the expedition the ships are being loaded for the return journey. Egyptians and Puntites work side by side as baskets of myrrh and frankincense, bags of gold and incense, ebony, elephant tusks, panther skins and a troop of excited monkeys are taken on board.

Punt was particularly rich in myrrh, which the Egyptians used to manufacture incense. Incense was always in demand. It was burned in great quantities during the daily temple rituals, and employed in the formulation of perfumes, the mummification of the dead, the fumigation of houses, and in medical prescriptions, where those suffering from bad breath were advised to chew balls of myrrh. The Punt brands of incense were highly prized, but could not be found in any great quantity within Egypt's borders where trees of any kind were rare.

The falling star that burns up the village of giant snakes is hard to explain. If it has to be based in reality, it might perhaps be a reference to a falling meteorite. The *benben* stone, a potent religious symbol housed in the temple of Re at Heliopolis, is also believed to have been a meteorite. The sole survivor of this tragedy promises the sailor, another sole survivor, that he will soon find his way home, and that he will eventually be buried in proper Egyptian style in his local cemetery. This would have been a promise of immense comfort to the sailor. Egyptians firmly believed that Egypt was the best land in the world. All Egyptians aimed to be buried in their homeland, where they knew that they would be accorded the funeral rites that would assure them eternal life.

The reader is invited to compare the loquacity of the attendant with the silence of the High Official. In Egypt, eloquence was always appreciated. But the story ends with an unanswerable question posed by the hitherto silent Official. "Who would give water to a goose that is about to be slaughtered?" Water is plentiful in Egypt and there is no obvious reason why one would not give water to a sacrificial goose, but it seems that the High Official is convinced that he is about to die. Whether or not this harsh punishment is justified - whether or not the king is a cruel taskmaster who rules over a land devoid of justice - we cannot tell, because we do not know what the High Official has or has not done.

7

THE TALKATIVE PEASANT

Once upon a time there lived a simple farmer named Khun-Anup. Khun-Anup dwelt in the Wadi Natrun with his wife Meryet and their children. He was a hard-working and decent man; his children were well fed, his wife was happy and his barn was filled to the rafters with valuable local produce. One day Khun-Anup called his wife to him.

"Our supplies of food are getting low. The time has come for me to travel to Egypt to trade my produce for food. Go to the barn, and see how much barley we have left from last year's harvest."

So Meryet went to the barn, and measured out twenty-six gallons of grain. This Khun-Anup divided into two unequal heaps. Twenty gallons would provide ample food for his family while he was away. The remaining six gallons were to be made into the bread and beer that would serve as his rations for the journey. And this was done.

Khun-Anup set off southwards on his travels, heading towards Neni-Nesut. His heart was light though his load was heavy, and his donkeys were making good speed under the weight of a vast array of goods. There were rushes, grasses and rare plants, natron and salt, precious woods, animal pelts including panther and jackal skins, many types of fowl, and much, much more besides. Eventually the small caravan reached the district of Per-Fefi, to the north of Medenit. And there, standing on the riverbank, Khun-Anup first encountered the man named Nemty-Nakht, an employee of the High Steward Rensi, son of Meru.

Nemty-Nakht, an unscrupulous and incurably lazy man, ran a practised eye over Khun-Anup's merchandise. He recognised the value of the load at once, and wished with all his greedy heart that he had a magic charm that would allow him to hijack the goods there and then. But he had no such charm, and was forced to fall back on his wits if he wanted to commit such an outrageous crime. Which of course he did. After a great deal of thought Nemty-Nakht smiled in triumph. He had devised a plan cunning enough to strip the naive peasant of all his precious goods and his donkeys as well. Running ahead of Khun-Anup, he spread a shawl across the narrow public road that ran in front of his house.

Khun-Anup, happily jogging along on the lead donkey, found that his path suddenly narrowed until it was no wider than a shawl. To one side of him there lapped the waters of the canal; to the other there was a field of growing barley; in the distance there was a house - the house of Nemty-Nakht. And in front of him there was indeed a shawl, spread across the road so that its fringe dipped into the canal water and its hem lay on the earth of the barley field. Standing beside the shawl was Nemty-Nakht, an unpleasant smile on his lips. Nemty-Nakht spoke first, his tone carelessly offensive.

"Take care, peasant. For I absolutely forbid you to step on my valuable shawl. And," he added, as Khun-Anup attempted to reverse his donkeys so that he might go round the garment via the field, "I also forbid you to step on my precious barley."

As the other side of the road was bordered by the canal, Khun-Anup now had no way forward. He tried to reason with Nemty-Nakht.

"My way is completely blocked. I cannot go into the water, the field is forbidden to me, and you are obstructing the road with your shawl. Will you not lift it, so that I may pass by?"

But even as Khun-Anup spoke, one of his donkeys lowered its head and ate an ear of barley from the field. This was exactly what Nemty-Nakht had been hoping for.

"This is an outrage! You have deliberately allowed your miserable donkey to eat my valuable barley. Now, peasant, I will seize your donkey as compensation. It will pay for its crime by working for me."

Khun-Anup, baffled by this ridiculous turn of events but still courteous, immediately made an offer of reasonable payment for the ear of barley eaten by his donkey. But Nemty-Nakht was deaf to reason. Seizing a green tamarisk rod he thrashed poor Khun-Anup until he cried out in pain, then he drove all the donkeys and their goods away to his own stables. The peasant was left alone on the road, his loud sobs only stifled by Nemty-Nakht's threat of murder should he make a fuss about his treatment.

Nemty-Nakht expected to hear no more from the intimidated peasant. But Khun-Anup knew his rights and was not prepared to let the matter drop. After a week spent pleading with Nemty-Nakht for the return of his property he travelled to the city of Neni-Nesut to appeal in person to Rensi, son of Meru, High Steward and employer of Nemty-Nakht. Khun-Anup told Rensi all that had happened, and Rensi was appalled by the injustice. He laid the matter before the local magistrates expecting them to support Khun-Anup, but they were inclined to take a different view.

"This story can't possibly be right. Nemty-Nakht is one of us, a gentleman. He would never steal from an honest man. This miserable complainant must be one of Nemty-Nakht's own peasants, who has been caught out in wrongdoing and who is trying to take revenge on a decent master. Why should we punish a good man like Nemty-Nakht over such a trivial matter? If he is asked to replace a few grains of salt, he will do so."

Rensi, son of Meru listened to this unfair judgement, but made no comment.

The peasant Khun-Anup lodged a formal appeal with Rensi, son of Meru. He spoke with great eloquence before him.

"If you go down to the river of truth you will sail on it with a fair wind. Your boat will remain sound and whole, and you will not capsize. You will not have to look upon the dark face of fear. Instead fine fish will swim to you and plump birds will fly to you. For you are the guardian of the unprotected. You are father to the orphan, husband to the widow, and brother to the abandoned wife. And your name will be remembered forever. For you are a great man, free of all avarice and greed, who ensures that right triumphs over evil. Allow me justice, O Lord. Take away my grief and listen to my plea, for I have been sorely wronged."

Rensi, amazed by what he had heard, referred the matter straight to King Nebkaure.

"Your Majesty, I have discovered an amazing thing, an uneducated peasant who is nevertheless capable of truly beautiful speech. This man came before me because he had been robbed and he wanted justice. I thought that it would amuse you to hear his words."

The king, fascinated by Rensi's tale, replied.

"If you wish me well, detain this talkative peasant. Do not respond to his pleas for, if you do not reply, he will be forced to carry on speaking. Have his words written down, and send them to me so that I may learn everything that he says. But do not be cruel. Make sure that the peasant is well fed - give him food without letting him know who provides it. And send food to his family, for peasants come to Egypt to trade their goods only when their larders are empty at home."

So Khun-Anup was provided with ten loaves of bread and two jugs of beer every day. This ration came, not direct from the hand of Rensi, but via a friend so that the peasant would not know who was feeding him. And Rensi wrote in secret to the mayor of Wadi Natrun, asking him to provide Khun-Anup's family with three baskets of grain each day.

The time came for the peasant Khun-Anup to make a second appeal before Rensi, son of Meru. This time Khun-Anup spoke with equal fluency but in less flattering terms.

"Great High Steward, richest of the rich, you are the dependable rudder of heaven and the plumb bob of the scales that carry the weight of truth. Do not be swayed from justice. A truly great man will take only ownerless property, and you have all you need for your own satisfaction. Surely you will agree that it is wrong that a balance may be allowed to tilt, or a plumb bob stray from the straight and narrow? But look around you. Justice flees from you, the magistrates are dishonest and all speech is twisted away from its original meaning. He who should punish the wrongdoers is now causing trouble himself...."

At this point Rensi, son of Meru interrupted the speechmaker with a threat of arrest which Khun-Anup, unstoppable in mid-flow, ignored.

"Yes, you are strong and mighty. But your heart is greedy and you show no mercy. How miserable is the wretched man whom you have destroyed. You are a messenger of the crocodile, you are worse than Sekhmet, Lady of Pestilence.

"The wealthy man should always be merciful. Violence should be left to criminals, and robbery to those who have nothing. We cannot reproach the poor robber as he is merely seeking to provide for himself (as indeed I myself may need to provide for myself if I lose all my goods). But you have enough food to make you vomit, and enough beer to make you drunk. You are rich in all kinds of treasure... Straighten your tongue, don't tell lies, and warn the magistrates to behave. Wisest of all men, do not ignore my case."

Rensi, following orders, heard this remarkable spate of words without making any response, and declined to make any sort of judgement. Khun-Anup, growing increasingly frustrated and bitter, was driven to following Rensi on a daily basis, appealing again and again against his harsh treatment at the hands of the court. On one occasion, pushed too far, Rensi ordered a casual beating for his impolite petitioner, but otherwise he remained impassive and gave no sign of listening. Eventually the desperate Khun-Anup was making his ninth appearance before the silent Rensi. And all this time, unbeknown to him, his words were being copied down so that they might be sent to the king.

On this occasion the desperate Khun-Anup did not mince his words.

"My Lord, High Steward, the tongue is a scale that will always betray men's deficiencies. Truth will out. He who benefits from falsehood has no heirs; his boat will not harbour at the mooring place. Do not be heavy, and do not be light. Do not be late, yet do not hurry. Do not turn your face away from one you know, nor be blind to one you have seen. Above all, do not betray the one who petitions you now. Abandon your reticence and speak. I have spent many hours pleading with you, but you have not listened to me. I shall now go and plead about you before Anubis."

On hearing this, Rensi sent two men to bring the peasant to him. Khun-Anup was afraid that he had said too much too often, and that he would be punished for his rudeness. But Rensi, speaking at last, quickly set his mind at rest:

"Do not be afraid my friend, but stay here with me and listen to all your petitions".

And to Khun-Anup's great amazement a scribe read out his words just as they had been copied down on nine lengthy papyrus scrolls. The scrolls were then sent to the court, where they gave King Nebkaure great pleasure.

The king ordered Rensi, son of Meru to pass judgement. And Rensi found in Khun-Anup's favour. Nemty-Nakht was arrested, and all his goods confiscated and passed to the peasant whose eloquence had earned him the respect of the king.

It is finished...

COMMENTARY ON
THE TALKATIVE PEASANT

The Talkative Peasant is a Middle Kingdom composition preserved in snatches on four separate and incomplete papyri, two of which also tell *The Story of Sinuhe.* Here all four have been combined to recreate one whole story. The tale is full of literary flourishes, repetitions and now-opaque puns and wordplays designed to appeal to an educated elite readership. But a text that seemed vibrant and absorbing to its intended audience can appear tediously repetitive to the modern reader. In order to spare the modern reader the full weight of Khun-Anup's lengthy oratory, petitions three - eight have here been condensed.

This is a potentially dull story, with just one moment of high drama. It has none of the excitement of magic, or travel to foreign lands and long-gone times found in our other Tales of Men, and it sets out to instruct rather than entertain. It is saved by the extreme loquaciousness of Khun-Anup, an innocent and ill-educated man of humble origins who knows his rights and never shuts up.

Khun-Anup is a frustrated, over-emotional peasant making a fuss about a relatively trivial matter. In contrast, the High Steward Rensi, son of Meru, is a restrained, self-controlled member of the elite who, acting under strict royal orders, communicates through silence. His silence could be mistaken for indifference or contempt, but it actually serves as a spur to Khun-Anup's speechmaking, and Rensi (and of course the audience/reader) knows this. All this must have been highly amusing to those accustomed to the frustrating and tortuously slow machinations of the Egyptian bureaucracy. The story carries a twofold message. In Egypt, justice or *maat* will always prevail; the king will ensure that this happens. And, as we have already seen in *The Shipwrecked Sailor*, there will always be an appreciation of eloquent speech.

Here we are shown a darker side to the glowing, sunny Egypt so often pictured on tomb walls. It is an Egypt of casual thefts, corruption and careless brutality, a land where the elite think nothing of ordering a casual beating for an inferior who has offended them. It is a land that needs a firm legal system to uphold the rights of the downtrodden.

Ancient Egypt recognised two broad classes of crime. Criminal offences - regicide, theft from the temples and palaces, and tomb robbing - were serious matters. As such they would be dealt with by the state, which clamped down hard on crimes with a formidable array of physical punishments at its disposal.

Here we are looking at a civil offence, a crime against a private person, which would not, under normal circumstances, be of any interest to the state legal system. Ideally a downtrodden private person needs a patron to support his cause and ensure that he receives justice. As we can see, Khun-Anup is very much on his own in his quest for justice and it is only by chance that the First Intermediate Period King Nebkaure becomes involved in his case. Nebkaure is a monarch who, like Snefru before him, seeks amusement through the spoken and subsequently written word. There is a certain amount of cruelty in Nebkaure's justice; although he has the commonsense to realise that the peasant's family must be in need of food, he appears completely indifferent to the mental stress caused to poor Khun-Anup.

It was the right of any Egyptian man or woman to petition an official and to place a civil action before the local court, a tribunal made up of respected citizens. There was no jury, and no professional lawyers. Nor was there any official help in catching miscreants. The plaintiff was very much responsible for the presentation of his or her own case; he or she was required to provide details of the dispute, the names of witnesses and, of course, the name of the defendant. This must have been a daunting responsibility for an ill-educated peasant in dispute with a social superior. As we can see in Khun-Anup's own case, the instinct of the upper class tribunal members was to believe their own kind. To make things worse, the courts were both slow to make judgement and almost incapable of enforcement. In one celebrated real-life case recorded at the workmen's village of Deir el-Medina, Thebes, a disagreement over a pot of fat took an almost unbelievable eighteen years to resolve. Here, as in *The Dispute of Horus and Seth*, another slow-moving legal wrangle, Egyptian justice triumphs in the end.

Khun-Anup and his family live in the Wadi Natrun, an oasis famous for its precious natron salt, a key ingredient in the mummification process. He is a trader rather than a farmer, and he is clearly wealthy. He owns a valuable string of donkeys and has an impressive range of luxury goods. But he dwells on the outskirts of Egypt - the very edge of the civilised world - and so he appears as something of a country bumpkin to the sophisticated city-dwelling officials he meets in his quest for justice. Unfortunately we are not able to translate many of Khun-Anup's goods. In the absence of coinage, he is obliged to barter his produce for foodstuffs, a system that served Dynastic Egypt well for many centuries.

His journey takes him from the Wadi towards the Middle Egyptian city of Neni-Nesut (Herakleopolis), the capital city of the 9th and 10th Dynasties. Medenit is the twenty-second nome, or province, of Upper Egypt. Per-Fefi is today unknown.

8

THE STORY OF SINUHE

This tale is told by the courtier Sinuhe, Count, Commander and Governor of Pharaoh's eastern territories, and most loyal and beloved friend of the king.

I was an attendant who waited on his lord, a servant of the royal harem assigned to the Princess Nefru, wife of King Senwosret and daughter of King Amenemhat.

Day 7 of the third month of the inundation, Year 30.
On this dreadful day the King of Upper and Lower Egypt, Amenemhat I, died suddenly. His spirit ascended to heaven. It flew upwards into the blue sky to become one with the golden sun disk, and the divine king and his creator were merged into one unique being. Egypt was stunned, and fell silent in her grief. The great palace doors were shut, the nobles mourned without restraint and the common people wept in the streets.

A short time before his death, King Amenemhat had sent a military expedition to the Western Desert under the command of his eldest son, Prince Senwosret. Their brief had been to smite the foreign lands and punish the disrespectful Libyan nomads. This campaign had proved a great success and Senwosret, ignorant of his father's death, was soon on his way home bringing with him many prisoners and a vast herd of captive cattle. I too had a place on that mission.

The palace officials sent their fastest messengers to intercept Senwosret on the western border. That night they found the prince and his companions camped by the road. Senwosret did not hesitate. He flew off to the palace, swift as a falcon, taking his most loyal attendants with him but leaving his army, and me, behind.

Senwosret had left behind a secret message for the royal sons who had accompanied him on his mission. One of the princes received the dreadful news while I was standing on duty close by, and I was able to eavesdrop on the conversation between the prince and the messenger. The words that I overheard had a terrible effect on me. My mind went blank, my heart pounded in my chest and I trembled from head to foot. At once I knew that I was not safe in Egypt. I had to flee; I had to find somewhere to hide.

To think was to act. I hid myself behind two bushes, then I started my long and lonely journey southwards.

Imagining scenes of desperate riot and bloodshed, I steered clear of the palace. I was scared that I might die there, just as the king had died. Instead I travelled along the edge of the western desert, reaching the Isle-of-Snefru. Here I spent some time hiding on the edge of the cultivation. At daybreak I set off again. I met a man who greeted me politely on the road, but I was too scared to respond to his courtesy. At suppertime I reached the jetty and, with the help of the west wind, was able to make the crossing in a rudderless boat. I then passed to the east of the quarries of the Red Mountain, and walked northwards until I reached Walls-of-the-Ruler, a mighty fortress built to repel the Asiatics and crush the desert nomads. Here I squatted behind another bush, hiding from the guards high up on the fortress walls.

At night I left the security of my bush and made for Peten, stopping at Isle-of-Kem-Wer. But here I collapsed. Desperate with thirst, I could go no further. My lips were blistered and my throat so parched from lack of water that I thought my end had come. Just as I resigned myself to death I heard the welcome sound of lowing cattle and, raising my eyes from the sand, saw a caravan of

Bedouin. With the greatest of good fortune their leader, who had visited Egypt before, recognised me. He gave me water and boiled milk and took me to live with his tribe. These were good people.

I travelled to Byblos and returned via Qedem, spending many happy months there. Then Ammunenshi, Chief of Upper Retenu, summoned me to him. He had heard of my integrity, intelligence and high position, and he wanted to quiz me over recent events in Egypt. Exactly why had I left my beloved homeland in such a hurry? I told him what had happened, but guardedly, because the news of the king's death had not officially been broken to me. I was, however, able to reassure him that, although I had been filled with such fear that I had run away, I had never been accused of any wrongdoing. I was not guilty of any crime, and I was not a wanted man. As to what had brought me to Retenu I was not sure - it was as if the gods themselves had directed my footsteps.

The chief asked me how Egypt would fare, deprived of her great King Amenemhat I. And I responded with a lengthy poem in praise of my former master Senwosret, who would now rule in his father's place. Senwosret was a much-loved and mighty prince; a fearless warrior who had already proved himself on the battlefield, yet a gentle and cultured man who was not afraid to show mercy to the weak and innocent. I urged Ammunenshi to write and introduce himself to Egypt's new king. For Senwosret would surely look kindly upon such a loyal ally.

Ammunenshi then turned his attention to me.

"Well it seems that Egypt is now happy under her new king. And you shall stay here and be happy with me. I will take care of you."

The chief was as good as his word. He married me to the most beautiful of his daughters, and allocated me a prime tract of land. This was a wonderful, fertile region named Yaa. There were fat figs on the trees, plump grapes on the vines, and more wine than water. There was no shortage of sweet honey, and olives by the basketful. The trees were loaded with fruits, the fields were ripe with golden grain, and there were many kinds of cattle. Ammunenshi made me a tribal chief. Generously, he ensured that I received a rich supply of foods. Every day, bread was baked for me, wine was brought to me, and meats were cooked for me - beef, and fowl and desert game caught especially for me. For pudding I had my choice of sweet and milky confections.

Here I spent many happy and prosperous years watching my sons grow into strong men. Each of my sons eventually became chief of his own tribe. Meanwhile my tent was famed for its hospitality. Envoys and travellers stayed with me. I gave water to the thirsty, directions to the lost, and help to those who had been robbed. When my father-in-law's territories were threatened I fought bravely on his behalf, carrying out numerous successful missions. I vanquished the hill tribes, plundered their cattle, seized their families and killed their men folk. For this service the Chief of Retenu loved me.

One day a man came to my tent to challenge me. He was a huge man, a man of unparalleled strength, the champion of his people. He meant to defeat me in combat and steal my goods and cattle. He had no personal grudge against me, beyond the fact that I was an Egyptian living in the land of the desert dwellers, yet he wanted to ruin me. I knew that I had to prove myself. Frightened though I was, I had no choice but to accept his challenge. That night I made my preparations. I strung my bow, checked my arrows, honed my dagger and polished my weapons.

When morning came I left the safety of my tent and saw that many people had gathered to watch our fight. I stood, inwardly quaking, in my allotted place. I knew that the crowds were on my side, and that gave me the courage that I so badly needed. The champion raised his battleaxe and shield, shot his arrows into the air and threw his javelins towards me. I stood firm, and by some miracle his weapons all missed their mark. Then, as the champion charged forward, I shot him just once in the neck. He screamed and fell forward onto his face, breaking his nose with a loud crunch. Seizing his axe, I cut off his head. And as the people shouted their appreciation, I gave a cry of triumph and offered thanks to the great Egyptian war god Montu.

Ammunenshi hugged me in his arms, weak with relief. Now I was able to plunder the champion just as he had planned to plunder me. I took all his cattle, and everything in his tent. In so doing I became wealthy beyond my wildest dreams. And I knew that at last the gods were pleased with me - my folly in fleeing Egypt had been forgiven. But just at the moment when I should have been at my happiest I felt a pang of longing for my homeland.

Many years passed. I grew older and more feeble; death was looming ever nearer. I sent up a prayer to whichever god had directed my footsteps eastwards. For I yearned to return home so that I might be mummified and buried in the traditions of my fathers. I did not want my body to be wrapped in the sheepskin of my adopted people. But having fled Egypt, I was too scared to return. I did not know what reception might await me.

My plight came to the attention of the King of Upper and Lower Egypt, Senwosret. And his heart was softened towards me. He sent me messages and gifts, and the royal children also sent me gifts. The king did not oppose my return for I may have acted foolishly, in the grip of my fear, but I had done no actual wrong. On the contrary, he begged me to return so that I might look forward to a proper Egyptian funeral, with its attendant rituals and promise of eternal life. "Sinuhe, think of your dead body, and come home."

This message reached me while I was standing in the midst of my tribe. So kind were the words of the great king to his servant that I threw myself to the ground and covered myself in dirt to demonstrate my humility. Then with great delight I replied to my lord, accepting his generous invitation to return.

I spent one more day in Yaa, ordering my affairs. My eldest son was to take over my position, and I left him all my goods and chattels - my servants, my herds and my fruit trees. Then I started my journey homewards, accompanied by my faithful Bedouin kinsmen. When I reached the Ways-of-Horus fort the commander of the garrison sent a message to the palace. An escort came to meet me, and there were ships full of precious gifts for the Bedouin who had cared for me for so many years. I embarked, and set sail for Egypt leaving my desert life behind me. And at daybreak I reached the capital city Itj-Tawy.

Ten men came to escort me to the king. At last I saw the mighty sphinxes at the palace entrance and I bowed low so that my head touched Egyptian soil. And here were the young royal children standing beside the doorway to greet me. I was taken to the great audience hall and stood at last before my king. He sat splendid on a carved throne beneath a golden canopy. I flung myself on the ground before his feet, and once again my wits left me. I could not look up, I could not hear properly. I could not speak. As the great lord uttered gentle words of welcome I could only quake with fear. His Majesty had to order a courtier to pick me up and support me while he spoke.

"Welcome home, Sinuhe. You have returned at last, after many years of roaming the foreign lands. You fled a young man, but old age has arrived and you are now looking forward to death. It is good that your body will eventually receive a proper Egyptian burial. But in the meantime, do not be frightened. Do not fear that you will be punished for your folly."

In a quiet voice, but with growing confidence, I somehow found the words to reply.

"I am not being disrespectful in my silence, my lord, but I am still very frightened. I am here now, and you must do with me as you wish. I place myself entirely in your hands."

The king summoned the queen and the royal princesses, and they rushed in to greet me as a long-lost friend - hesitating only slightly at my unkempt appearance for my beard and layers of desert dirt made me almost unrecognisable. They danced, sang, and shook their rattles, offering praise to Hathor for my return. Then they took me by the hand and led me from the audience chamber into the house of a prince. This seemed a house of great luxury to my weary, travel-worn eyes; it had a cool bathroom and mirrors, linen clothing, ointments, perfumes and servants to attend to my needs. I was washed, and the years fell from my body. I was shaved and my hair was cut so that I once again appeared as a true Egyptian gentleman. I was dressed in the finest linen and perfumed with the sweetest unguents. That night, I slept in a bed for the first time in years.

Through the mercy of the king I was given a house, a garden and a regular ration of food. Best of all, I was allocated a small stone pyramid in the middle of the royal cemetery. The royal masons built my pyramid, a master architect designed it and a master sculptor carved it. Inside there was a burial shaft, and all the goods necessary for the Afterlife. I was given mortuary estates, and mortuary priests to maintain my cult forever. And my statue was covered with gold and with electrum. Truly, no other commoner had been so blessed by his king. I remained the king's favourite until the day that I died.

It is finished, as has been found in writing....

COMMENTARY ON
THE STORY OF SINUHE

Sinuhe's story takes the form of an autobiography. Written in the first person in elegant prose with intermittent flights into poetry and quoted correspondence from the king, it is at first sight exactly the type of text that a high-ranking 12th Dynasty official might have carved or painted on his tomb wall. At second sight it is not so typical in its content. In particular, the negative plot developments that show Sinuhe in a less than heroic light are a clear indication that this tale belongs to the realm of fiction. No Egyptian of sense would include such damning negativity in his tomb. Fact or fiction, it was certainly a popular and much-copied story in its day, and we have several papyri and ostraca, dating from the Middle Kingdom to the New, which preserve extracts of varying length. These have here been combined to make one complete tale.

The underlying theme of the story is one very dear to the Egyptian heart. It is a non-Biblical exodus. Like *The Shipwrecked Sailor*, Sinuhe has travelled out of his normal environment. And he too has realised that there is no place like home. He yearns for the mummification and decent burial that will guarantee him eternal life beyond death, and he is prepared to abandon all the luxuries of his desert life - including his foreign-born children - in order to achieve his goal.

It is its real historical setting that makes this story so interesting to modern readers. For while Sinuhe is an entirely fictional being, Amenemhat I and his son Senwosret I are genuine Kings of Egypt. And contemporary documents confirm what Sinuhe is obviously too frightened, or to delicate, to spell out. Amenemhat, charismatic founder of the 12th Dynasty, was murdered. The original audience would have known this crucial fact. The death of a king was always a difficult moment for the Egyptians. If, as they believed, their king was a semi-divine being endorsed by the gods and essential to the maintenance of *maat*, how could he leave his people unprotected and vulnerable to chaos? In Egypt even the gods could die - the murder of Osiris tells us this - but the death of a god or a demi-god was a very bad thing indeed. The idea that someone might be prepared to challenge *maat* by deliberately killing the king was an almost unthinkable heresy.

Heresy or not, regicide did occasionally happen. Egypt must have been burdened with her fair share of violent extremists and loners, but kings were most vulnerable to their immediate family - those who were perhaps best placed to see the mortal man behind the god, and who had most to gain by his death. In this case we have an eye-witness account of the murder, apparently written by the victim! The *Instruction of King Amenemhat* is a lengthy, bitter letter addressed by the deceased Amenemhat to his son and heir Senwosret. Of course this is impossible; the letter was actually written some time after the event by the scribe Khety:

> *It was after supper and night had fallen. I was lying on my bed and resting, for I was weary. As I began to drift into sleep, the weapons that should have been used to protect me were turned against me. I awoke with a jump, alert for the fight, and found that it was a combat with the guard. Had I been able to seize my weapon I would have beaten back the cowards single-handed, but no one is strong at night. No one can fight alone and no success can be achieved without a helper.*

Our hero was far away from the palace when this terrible event occurred, and so can have had no direct involvement in the murder. Yet, in the few seconds it takes to eavesdrop on a private conversation, the horror-struck Sinuhe has abandoned his respected role of king's attendant and is to be found lurking in a most undignified fashion behind two bushes at the side of the road. The whole course of his life has been irredeemably changed for the worse. Chaos has replaced *maat*. Of course Sinuhe is a fictional character. He acts in this seemingly irrational way because his author makes him do so, and we need look no further for an explanation of his reaction. But if we go along with the pretence that he is real, we must ask why he is so very frightened. Amenemhat was an elderly man already in his 30th regnal year - his natural death was more or less imminent and would not have provoked such extreme terror. Does Sinuhe know that the king has been murdered? And is he somehow connected with the plot?

Meanwhile Senwosret, already acknowledged as co-regent to Amenemhat I, is also absent from the palace, subduing the Libyan nomads who are a constant irritation along the western border. On hearing the sad news he at once abandons his army and rushes back home to claim his inheritance. The proverb "he who buries, inherits" may not have had the force of law, but it was taken seriously, and the royal harem could have provided many brothers eager to step into Senwosret's sandals.

Sinuhe declares his intention to flee south. But in fact his chaotic journey takes him northeast, from the Libyan Desert, across the Nile, past Memphis (the location of the Isle-of-Snefru, which is not actually an island but a funerary estate), and over the Sinai land bridge. Here he follows the inhospitable 140-mile desert road, the Ways-of-Horus, into southern Canaan. On his journey, and again on his return, he passes the impressive mud-brick fortresses built to serve as combined garrisons and customs posts. Walls-of-the-Ruler is one of these fortresses, built by Amenemhat I to provide protection, water and provisions for those passing on legitimate business while discouraging the uncontrolled migration of Asiatics (a general term for Easterners). At Sile, the most westerly fortress, all parties wishing to cross the border were required to register by name, town of origin and destination, and all foreigners wishing to enter Egypt needed either an entry permit or a bribe.

Sinuhe is now an involuntary nomad. After a quick trip to the Syrian port of Byblos he travels through Qedem, most probably a forested area to the east of the Lebanese mountain range. Then he is summoned, or captured, by Ammunenshi, Chief of Upper Retenu, a region on the River Litani in Palestine. Luckily, Ammunenshi can speak Egyptian, and he takes a great shine to his visitor. Sinuhe becomes a family member, and settles in the fertile and possibly fictional land of Yaa.

Sinuhe's new life in Canaan is one of undeserved, and totally un-Egyptian, luxury. He now lives in a tent rather than a house; he has no bathroom, no fresh linen and no barber to shave his beard; the meats in this strange land are cooked in milk. His courage fully restored, Sinuhe gains wealth as a pastoralist and respect as a warrior. His life is as happy as any life away from Egypt can ever be. Only when the mighty challenger appears to try to rob him of all his goods is he reminded that he is a stranger in a strange land. We see the fleeting return of the old, frightened Sinuhe. But this time Sinuhe is determined to meet his fate face to face. In a battle scene strongly reminiscent of the tale of David and Goliath, which at the same time brings to mind the timeless scenes of pharaohs smiting unfortunate foreigners, he defeats his enemy with a single well-placed shot. In so doing, he gains increased riches and respect. His story then proceeds, with a startling abruptness, to a second Biblical theme. It becomes the parable of the prodigal son.

At the very moment of his triumph, Sinuhe realises that he must return to Egypt. He has retained his loyalty to his native gods, and he now gives thanks to Montu, the falcon-headed warrior god of Thebes. Montu, the southern equivalent of Re of Heliopolis, was one of the dominant gods of the Middle Kingdom. Eventually he would be displaced by his near neighbour and fellow war god Amen of Thebes, but the warrior kings of the New Kingdom, including Tuthmosis III and Ramesses II whose tales are told here, would continue to respect his prowess as a fighter.

Leaving Egypt is neither a good nor a desirable thing. Sinuhe escaped by means of a rudderless boat that he could not steer and a perverse western wind; in Egypt, the wind always blows boats southwards, while the river flows northwards. He then walked along the desert road, a long, hot journey that nearly killed him. His homeward journey is far more controlled; it is a journey from chaos to *maat*. He has an escort and a boat, complete with rudder, which sails swiftly to the palace at Itj-Tawy, the new capital city built by Amenemhat I close by his northern pyramid site of el-Lisht. Unfortunately Itj-Tawy, situated somewhere to the south of the Old Kingdom capital Memphis, is today lost.

The royal family, the queen and the curiously un-aged royal children, are shocked by Sinuhe's appearance. Not only is he old, he has become a bearded desert dweller, and it takes a lengthy session in the bathroom to restore him to the ideal of Egyptian manhood. Sinuhe is reborn. Clean, scented and appropriately dressed in white linen, he moves into a house and waits patiently for death. His self-inflicted sufferings are over and he is at peace, for his tomb, his house for eternity, is ready and waiting in the royal cemetery. His story has come full circle.

9

THE DOOMED PRINCE

Once upon a time, in a land far, far away, there lived an elderly king. This king had everything that a man could desire; health, wealth, a beautiful palace and a loving young wife. Yet he was sad, because he had no child, and he longed for a child more than anything in the world. The king prayed to his gods that his wife might give birth, and they agreed to grant his wish. That night the king visited his wife in her bedchamber, and she conceived. And nine months later her son was born, whole and healthy. The king was beside himself with happiness.

It was time for the Seven Hathors to decide the baby's fate. The palace was hushed as they stood by the crib, and spoke.

"He will meet his death through a dog, or through a snake, or maybe through a crocodile."

The nursemaids rushed straight to the king, and told him of the prophecy. And the king was instantly plunged into a deep sorrow. For he loved his baby son more than anything in the world, and he did not want him to die an untimely death.

Determined to protect the baby from his destiny, the king had a stone house built in the desert. The house was filled with expensive furniture, its storerooms piled high with good food and drink taken from the palace kitchens. It was staffed with loyal attendants chosen by the king himself. Here the prince would be raised apart from other children. He would never be allowed to play outside, and so would never come face to face with his fate, whatever it might be.

The years flew by and the pretty baby grew into a fine and sturdy boy, the pride of his father's heart. But the young prince was increasingly lonely; his days were tedious, his nights endless, and he longed for a companion. One day he was sitting on the roof of his house, idly watching the road below. And he saw a man walk by, followed by a greyhound. The boy was intrigued - he had never seen a dog before. Excited, he summoned his attendant, and demanded to know just what the strange four-legged creature could be.

"It is a greyhound dog, my lord."

"Have one just like it brought to me, now!"

Troubled, the attendant went straight to the king. And the king was torn in two. He had no wish to deny his son anything, but he wanted to protect him against his fate. After much deliberation he reluctantly ordered that a small puppy be brought to the prince "so that his heart will not grieve". And it was done.

Many more years passed and the fine boy became a fully-grown, exceptionally handsome man. A determined and logical man, who was no longer prepared to sit in isolation in his well-furnished house in the desert. The prince sent a message to his father.

"What is the point of my sitting here all alone? My fates have been foretold, and I cannot avoid them. Let me go free, so that I may live as I wish until the gods decide to do with me as they will."

The sorrowing king could see the sense of this argument. So a splendid chariot was prepared for the prince, equipped with an impressive range of weapons. And a servant was appointed to accompany the prince on his travels. The prince was ferried over the river to the eastern shore, and given his father's brief blessing. "Go wherever you wish."

The prince set off, free at last. And his faithful greyhound, now a full-grown dog, went with him.

The prince travelled northwards over the desert, following no particular path but riding wherever his heart took him and living off desert game. And at last he came to the far off land of Naharin.

Now the King of Naharin had only one child, a daughter. That daughter was more beautiful than any other woman in the world, and she was as sweet in nature as she was beautiful. Her father loved her deeply. Although she attracted many offers of marriage, he felt that only the most noble and athletic of men should be her husband. So he built for her a stone tower, whose window was seventy cubits from the ground. And here at the window the beautiful princess stood alone, looking down on the world below. The King of Naharin summoned her noble suitors to the base of the tower. All the unmarried princes of Syria arrived at the tower and listened as the King of Naharin spoke.

"Whoever jumps up to my daughter's window, he will win her hand in marriage."

The princes immediately started to leap upwards, competing to reach the window. They did this day after day, for they were each determined to win the hand of the beautiful princess.

Three months passed, and the vigorous young men continued to jump with undimmed enthusiasm. Eventually the Egyptian prince passed by on his travels. He halted, intrigued by the high tower and the jumping princes. The young men made the newcomer feel very welcome; they took him to their lodgings, bathed him, rubbed him with oils, bandaged his feet which had blistered from too much walking, and fed his horses, his dog and his attendant. Curious, they asked where he had come from. The prince, reluctant to reveal his true nobility, quickly made up a story.

"I am the son of an Egyptian charioteer. When my mother died my father took a new wife, a stepmother for me. She soon came to hate me and I could do nothing to please her. So I left home, fleeing from her harsh words."

This sorry tale stirred the sympathy of the leaping princes. They hugged the newcomer and kissed him, and begged him to feel at home with them.

The prince just had to ask: "Why do you spend every day leaping up towards that high window, lads?"

And they told him the whole story of the King of Naharin, his beautiful daughter and her impossible window. The Egyptian was eager to try to win the hand of the fair princess but he couldn't; his sore feet hurt too much. So he was forced to stand by and watch as his companions made their daily jumps. But unknown to him, high in her tower, the princess had her eye on the newcomer. For he was as handsome as she was fair, and she desired him as her husband.

A few days later the prince's feet were fully healed, and he was able to take his place amongst the leaping suitors. With one mighty bound he sailed through the air and reached the window of the Princess of Naharin. She was delighted. She kissed him, and held him in a close embrace. Meanwhile her attendants rushed to tell the king that his daughter's husband was found.

"Which high-born prince has reached my princess?" the king demanded.

His face fell as he realised that his precious daughter had been won, not by a noble prince, but by the lowly son of an Egyptian charioteer.

"I don't believe it! Do you really expect me to give my daughter to an Egyptian fugitive? Make him go away, at once!"

The attendants hurried back to the tower, and ordered the prince to leave Naharin immediately. But the headstrong princess heard their words, and grew angry.

"I swear by the great god Re-Horakhty. If my fiancé is taken away from me I shall not eat and I shall not drink. I shall die, straightaway."

Trembling, the attendants returned to the king and repeated his daughter's threat. The king sent men to slay the Egyptian, so that the matter would be over and done with once and for all. But again the princess realised what was happening, and again she took a vow.

"By the great god Re. If this man is killed, I too shall be dead before sunset. I shall not live a single hour without him."

Hearing these words, the King of Naharin realised that his determined daughter had outsmarted him. He summoned the couple to him, and was very impressed with what he saw. The Egyptian had an unexpected natural dignity; perhaps he would not make too bad a son-in-law after all. The king embraced the Egyptian and kissed him. "Tell me all about yourself, for now you are my son."

And, for reasons best known to himself, the prince repeated the invented story of the cruel stepmother and the flight from Egypt. Hearing this tale the King of Naharin gave his blessing to the match. And the happy couple were given a house and fields, cattle and all sorts of good things.

After many days the Egyptian prince told his wife the truth about his destiny. "I am fated to die by one of three animals; the dog, the snake or the crocodile."

Alarmed, she at once demanded that the prince's faithful greyhound be killed. But he refused to listen to her.

"How stupid. Why should I kill a dog that I myself have raised from a puppy? He is a lovely dog - my best friend. He wouldn't hurt a fly. He will certainly never harm me."

The wife, however, was not convinced, and she started to watch both her husband and his pet closely from that day onwards.

Now, unknown to the prince, the crocodile that was to be his fate had followed him from Egypt and was even now lurking in a lake in the village close by his house. There it was stuck, for there was also a strong daemon in the lake. The daemon would not let the crocodile leave the water, and the crocodile in turn would not let the daemon go for its daily stroll around the village. Every day, as soon as the sun rose, the crocodile and the daemon fought each other tooth and nail. And that had been happening for many months.

The next day was a holiday. The prince spent the whole day eating and drinking in his house; this so tired him out that he fell asleep that night as soon as his head touched his headrest. His wife, however, had drunk little and was still alert. She filled a bowl with wine, and a bowl with water, and then she sat and watched over her sleeping husband. Suddenly, without any warning, a snake slithered out of a small hole in the bedroom wall. It intended to bite the prince and so fulfil his destiny. But instead the snake drank from the wine bowl, and became sleepy and confused. As it collapsed in a drunken stupor the wife hacked it to pieces with a kitchen knife that she had laid ready for just such an emergency.

The noise of the snake-slaying woke the husband, who rather tetchily demanded to know what was going on. The wife was able to show him the pieces of snake littering the bedroom floor.

"Look, your god has delivered you from one of your fates. He will surely deliver you from the others, and you will be safe at last."

Hearing this, the prince made an offering to Re. He continued to praise Re for many days.

A few days after the curious incident of the snake in the night the prince went for a stroll round the village. Naturally, he took his faithful greyhound with him. His wife, however, chose to stay at home.

Suddenly, most alarmingly, his dog began to speak.

"I am your fate and you can't escape. Grrrrr!"

Hearing this, the prince took to his heels, running away from the growling dog straight towards the lake. Jumping into the water he had just one second to think himself safe before the crocodile seized him in its powerful jaws. To his absolute horror, the crocodile also spoke.

"I am your fate! I have followed you from Egypt so that I might kill you. But for many months I have been tormented by the strong daemon that lives in this lake. Now, I am prepared to strike a bargain with you. If I let you go, you must help me to kill the daemon that torments me daily."

When the next day dawned the daemon returned to the lake....

COMMENTARY ON
THE DOOMED PRINCE

This 18th/19th Dynasty fantasy offers elements found in modern fairy tales, and we can instantly recognise parts of Sleeping Beauty (the bad fairy at the christening) and Rapunzel (the princess immured in a high tower) within its plot. To the Egyptians the story echoed the themes of *Sinuhe* and *The Shipwrecked Sailor* (travel away from home) and even *The Destruction of Mankind* (the use of strong drink to deflect a destroyer).

Strongly plot-driven, and lacking detailed descriptive passages, the story holds the reader's attention - we really want to know if and how the anonymous prince escapes his fate, and how and when he reveals his true status to his new family. It is therefore unfortunate that it is preserved on just one papyrus, and that the end of the tale is missing. But it is perhaps not unduly optimistic to speculate, given the light-hearted tone of the piece, that the practical princess ensures that her beloved prince survives to enjoy a long and happy life. Maybe he even returns home, so that he can receive a traditional Egyptian burial. Certainly the fates, traditionally spoken by the seven forms of the goddess Hathor at every child's birth, were not considered inescapable and could be overcome by a judicious combination of luck, piety, justice and cunning. This is why some authors prefer to rename this tale *The Prince Who Knew His Fate*.

Seven was considered an important number signifying completeness or totality. Observant readers will remember that the Metternich Stela tells us how the goddess Isis was accompanied on her travels by seven scorpions, while in the *Five Magical Tales* Webaoner makes a wax crocodile seven fingers long which he turns into a living crocodile seven cubits long. The crocodile then keeps the wife's lover under the water for seven days.

The prince journeys eastwards from Egypt, across the Sinai land bridge, to the faraway but real land of Naharin (more commonly known as Mitanni) on the upper Euphrates River. He travels by chariot - confirmation of the age of this version of the story, as the horse-driven chariot was a New Kingdom development.

10

THE TWO BROTHERS

Once upon a time there were two brothers, born to the same mother and the same father. The elder brother was named Anubis, and the younger brother was named Bata. Anubis was a prosperous man. He had a fine house, a fertile farm and a beautiful wife. Because their parents were dead, the young Bata lived with Anubis and his wife. Anubis cared for Bata as a father cares for a son, and Bata in turn worked hard for his brother, herding his cattle, ploughing his fields and harvesting his grain. Bata was an excellent and exceptionally handsome young man; there was none so fine in the whole of Egypt.

Bata had a daily routine. He would rise at dawn and head for the fields with the cattle. Returning home at nightfall he would bring armfuls of good things; vegetables, milk and wood. These he would give to Anubis as he sat with his beautiful wife in the cool house. Bata would then eat his evening meal, and leave to sleep in the barn with the animals. This could have been a lonely life, but Bata was content. For Bata had an unusual gift, one that he kept secret from his brother. He was able to speak to the cattle. By listening to their conversation he was able to find the best grazing lands, and so the cattle under his charge became the fattest and most fertile cattle in the land.

When the time came to plough the fields and sow the seeds, Anubis left the house to work alongside Bata. The two brothers ploughed with a light heart, happy to be working together under the warm Egyptian sun. But then Anubis realised that they had not brought enough seed with them. And he sent Bata home to bring some more.

Arriving at the house, Bata found his brother's beautiful wife lounging in the cool courtyard, languidly playing with her long, dark hair. She smiled up at him and he, disconcerted, blurted out his instructions.

"Get up and fetch me some seed, for Anubis is waiting in the fields. Don't dawdle."

But the wife made no move save to stroke her long, dark tresses with her elegant fingers.

"Go to the grain-store and fetch what you need yourself. Don't interrupt my toilette."

And so Bata went to the store and filled a large vessel with seed. Hoisting the load onto his shoulder, he turned to leave the house. Once again he had to pass close by his sister-in-law, and he saw that her hairstyle was now complete.

"How much grain are you carrying there?" she asked in a low, husky voice.

Puzzled, Bata replied: "three measures of wheat and two measures of barley, that is all. Why?"

"Mmm..." the wife continued, running an appraising glance over his glistening torso, "what well-developed muscles you have, and how strong you must be. I have been watching you work in the fields for many days, your bare chest exposed to the sun...." and her fine dark eyes grew misty with lust. To Bata's intense alarm, she jumped to her feet and took hold of his arm, pinching his firm flesh as she did so.

"Come, let me loosen my hair. And let us spend an hour or so lying together. You will enjoy it. And afterwards I will make you some fine new clothes."

This proposal filled the honest Bata with a rage that he could not hide, and his wanton sister-in-law trembled before him.

"No! How can you say such things? You have been like a mother to me, and my beloved brother has been my father. You took me in as a child, and raised me. What you have suggested is repugnant to me. Never mention it again. And I in turn swear that I will not let one word of this disgraceful matter pass my lips."

And turning on his heels he ran to the fields and resumed his work alongside Anubis.

Back at the house, the faithless wife grew increasingly frightened. What if Bata were to tell Anubis of her attempted seduction? She must put her side of the story first. Quickly she smeared dark fat over her body and applied bandages so that she looked like the victim of a severe assault. And when Anubis returned home, leaving Bata to finish off the work in the fields, she did not run to greet him as she usually did, and she did not bring the water to wash his hands. She had not lit the lamp, so the house was in darkness. Peering through the gloom, Anubis found his beautiful wife retching and groaning on her bed. Obviously she had been attacked. Anubis was horrified.

"Who has done this terrible thing to you? Tell me at once and I will seek revenge."

He had to bend low to catch the one, treacherous name.

"Bata!"

Seeming to rally slightly, the wife told her poisonous tale. "It happened while you were happily working in the fields. Your brother came to the house to fetch some seed, and he saw me sitting alone. He ordered me to lie with him, but of course I would not - I would never betray you, my husband. So he beat me, to stop me telling you this sorry tale. Now, if you let him live, I shall surely die. You must kill him at once, when he comes home."

Anubis was filled with the hot rage of a southern panther. He sharpened his spear to a fine point, then stood patiently behind the barn door, waiting for Bata's return. And, as night fell, Bata did indeed make his way back to the barn, his arms loaded with produce and his cattle walking before him. But as the first cow entered the barn she stopped, and spoke.

"Be very careful Bata. Your brother Anubis is hiding behind the door, and he intends to kill you with his spear. You must run away."

A second cow entered behind the first, and spoke the very same words.

"Be very careful Bata. Your brother Anubis is hiding behind the door, and he intends to kill you with his spear. You must run away."

Mystified, Bata looked under the door, and caught a glimpse of his brother's feet. Realising that the cows were speaking the truth, he dropped his load and fled. And Anubis, enraged, charged after him.

Bata prayed aloud as he ran from his murderous brother.

"Great god Re, you can distinguish right from wrong. Help me now."

And Re, moved by Bata's plight, caused a mighty river of crocodile-infested water to spring up between the two men. There they stood facing each other in the gathering gloom, one on the left bank, and one on the right. Anubis was furious with himself, for he had failed to kill Bata. Bata, still shaking with fear, shouted across the watery divide.

"Wait there, and when daylight comes we will sort this matter out, with the sun as our witness. Re will tell you who is guilty and who is innocent. Then I shall leave your house and be with you no more, for I shall travel to the Valley of the Cedar."

Eventually the long night ended and the sun's disk rose into the pale blue sky. The two brothers stared hollow-eyed at each other across the waters, and Bata asked his brother why he had attempted to murder him without listening to his side of the story.

"For when you sent me to fetch that wretched seed, your slut of a wife attempted to seduce me. I resisted her, yet somehow, in your eyes, the true sequence of events has been distorted."

He told Anubis the whole, sorry tale, ending with an oath shouted out loud before the great sun god Re:

"You have no reason to kill me, save the word of a dirty whore".

And taking a reed dagger, Bata hacked off his own penis and threw it into the water.

A catfish swallowed the penis, and Bata grew fevered and weak from loss of blood. Anubis, stranded on the opposite bank, could only weep for his young brother, for now he believed his story, but could not cross the crocodile-infested waters to comfort him. Then Bata cried out again in his anguish.

"You find it easy enough to believe ill of me - can you not search your heart and remember some good deed that I have done for you instead? Go back to your home, and look after your precious wife and cattle. For I can no longer live with you, but must go to the Valley of the Cedar. But, I ask just one thing of you, my brother. If you learn that something bad has happened to me, come and look for me. I shall take out my heart, and place it in the blossom of the topmost bough of the tallest cedar tree in the Valley. If that tree should fall, come and search for my heart. Do not stop looking, even if it takes you seven years or more. And when you find it, place it in a bowl of cool water. If you do that I will live again to avenge those who have wronged me. You will know that something bad has happened to me when the jug of beer in your hand starts to foam and froth. Do not ignore this sign, but come at once to help me."

Bata turned away from the water, and set off on his lonely journey to the Valley of the Cedar. And Anubis wiped away his tears and returned home grieving, his hands raised to his head and his skin smeared with the mud of mourning. He killed his faithless wife at once, and threw her body to the dogs. Then he squatted in a corner, and brooded over his loss.

After many days Bata reached the Valley of the Cedar where he spent his days hunting game in the desert. At night he always returned to sleep beneath the great tree that held his heart. Soon, his strength restored, he started to build himself a house besides the great pine, for he longed to find a good woman and start a family. Bata's house was splendid, filled with many valuable things, and there in all the splendour he lived, alone and lonely.

One day Bata left his house to take a stroll in the Valley. Here he met the Ennead - the nine great gods - as they walked about, ruling the world. The gods felt sorry for Bata, and stopped to speak to him.

"O Bata, the lies told by your brother's wife have caused you to flee your home town, and now you live here all alone, isolated from your family and friends. But cheer up, Anubis has killed his faithless wife, and thus you are revenged."

Understanding Bata's deep loneliness, Re ordered the creator god Khnum to make a companion for him, and this the god did. The girl that Khnum made for Bata was more beautiful and more fragrant than any woman in the entire land. Then the Seven Hathors came to forecast her fate. With one voice they spoke.

"She shall die by the executioner's blade."

The beautiful young girl moved into Bata's splendid house, and into his heart. He desired her with every fibre of his being; his love frightened her in its intensity. But he had cut off his penis, and was impotent, and his bride remained a virgin. On his orders the girl spent her days in the shade of his house while he went out into the hot sun, hunting game for them both to eat. The girl was bored and chafed against her confinement, but Bata would not allow her to go outside, for he was worried that she might be snatched by the cruel sea. "If that were to happen, I could not rescue you, for I am a woman just like you. I tell you this, though. My heart lies in the blossom of the topmost bough of the tallest cedar tree in the Valley. If anyone finds it there, I shall fight him to the death."

Bata, relieved to be able to talk after many months of loneliness, confided to his beautiful companion all the innermost secrets of his heart.

One long hot, dull day, while Bata was, as usual, out hunting, the bored young girl was tempted outside. As she strolled, innocently enjoying the shade of the great pine tree, she was horrified to see the sea surging towards her. She ran for the safety of the house, and nearly made it, but the sea called out to the pine tree "Catch her for me".

The pine tree snatched a lock of the girl's dark hair, and gave it to the sea. The sea carried this lock of hair all the way to the Nile, and dropped it in the waters used by the palace washermen. And thus the scent of the young girl's hair perfumed the King of Egypt's clothes.

No one could imagine what the exotic new scent might be. The king quizzed the washermen, who angrily denied using any new products. Everyone remained baffled until the chief laundryman discovered the lock of perfumed hair still floating in the waters of the washing pool. The king's most learned scribes soon identified the tress.

"It is the hair of the most beautiful girl ever made, a daughter of Re fashioned by the gods. It has been sent to you as a greeting. Send your men to search the whole world for her. Look everywhere, but pay particular attention to the Valley of the Cedar. You can collect this treasure, and she shall be yours."

And so it was done. The king's men set out to search the whole world and came back empty handed; only the men sent to the Valley of the Cedar failed to return. There was good reason for this. Bata, frantic to protect his way of life, had killed the soldiers, leaving only one alive.

The King of Egypt tried again. This time he sent not only troops and chariots, but also an older, experienced woman who could tempt the unworldly young girl with clothing, jewellery and feminine trinkets the like of which she had never seen. The woman was successful in her mission, and the troops returned with the beautiful but sadly fickle young girl. The old King of Egypt was absolutely delighted with his prize. He married the young girl, and made her his queen. Then he quizzed her about her former life with Bata, but all she would say was "Cut down and chop up the great cedar tree that grows outside his house".

The king's troops returned to the Valley of the Cedar and hacked down the great tree that held Bata's heart. Instantly, Bata fell down dead.

The very next day, far away, life was progressing as normal. Anubis came home from the fields, washed his hands, and called for a jug of beer for he was thirsty after a hard day's work under the hot sun. But as soon as the beer was placed in his hands it started to foam and froth. Alarmed, Anubis called for a jug of wine and watched with horror as it turned sour in his grasp. Then he knew what he must do. He packed his bag, laced his sandals, took up his staff and set off for the Valley of the Cedar. Here he soon found his brother's house and, inside, his beloved brother lying dead on his bed. Anubis wept long and hard over Bata's body. Then he set to work. For three years he searched in vain for Bata's heart. Just as he was about to give up he found a pinecone, and somehow he knew that this was the thing he had been searching for. Anubis dropped the pinecone into a bowl of cool water, and then sat beside Bata's bier to watch what might happen.

As night fell the heart inside the cone absorbed the water and Bata's stiff body shuddered and jerked. Bata's dead eyes rolled towards his brother, and Anubis held out the bowl so that Bata might drink from it. Thus Bata's heart made its way to its proper place, and Bata came alive again. The brothers embraced each other, and talked throughout the night. For Bata had a plan to revenge himself on those who had betrayed him.

"I shall transform myself into a bull, the most beautiful, multi-coloured bull ever seen, and you can ride upon my back. By sunrise we will have reached the new home of my faithless wife. You must present me to the King of Egypt. He will welcome the gift of the splendid bull, and you will receive a great reward. You can then return home, leaving me behind to obtain my revenge."

The plan was carried out in every detail. The King of Egypt was enormously pleased with the magnificent gift, and Anubis was soon on his way home laden with the weight of the bull in silver and gold. Meanwhile Bata remained in the palace disguised as the multicoloured bull. As the king's favourite, he was permitted to roam from room to room at will.

One day the bull entered the kitchen where the king's beautiful young wife stood. And he began to talk to her.

"See, despite all your efforts, I am still alive."

"Who are you?" gasped the queen, horrified.

"I am Bata. I know that it was you who told the king to chop down the cedar tree, and I know that you must have done this because you wanted me dead. But look, I am alive again. Not a man this time, but a bull."

Hearing this, the queen ran from the kitchen in abject terror.

The King of Egypt sat down to a splendid banquet with his beautiful young wife. The girl poured the old man many goblets of wine, and he grew increasingly pleased with her attentions. Then she murmured in a low, sweet voice:

"Husband, will you promise me something before the gods?"

"Anything you want, sweetheart."

"I want you to sacrifice the great multicoloured bull that wanders around the palace, and I want to eat his liver. After all, he is a beast with no practical use."

The king heard these words with a heavy heart, for he was fond of his magnificent bull, but a promise was a promise. So the next day he ordered his steward to make the sacrifice. The bull was killed, and as he died two drops of blood flew from his neck. One landed on the left doorpost of the palace, and one landed on the right. Instantly, two tall persea trees grew from the blood and stood straight and beautiful before the palace. This marvel caused great celebrations throughout the whole of Egypt, and the king himself rode out in his golden chariot to view the trees. The beautiful young queen, too, came out to see the wonder. And as the king sat in the shade of one tree, she sat under the other. Then Bata spoke again to his wife.

"Greetings, faithless one. I am your husband, Bata. In spite of all you have done, I am still alive. I know that it was you who told the king to chop down the cedar tree, and I know that it was you who told the king to sacrifice the magnificent bull. You can only have done such a cruel thing because you want me dead."

The desperate queen knew what she had to do. A few days later, as she again poured wine for her doting husband, she spoke in a low, sweet voice:

"Husband, will you promise me something before the gods?"

"Anything you want, sweetheart."

"I want you to cut down the two great persea trees that stand at the portal of the palace, and I want you to use their wood to make exquisite furniture for me."

The king listened with a heavy heart, for he was fond of his beautiful trees, but a promise was a promise. So the next day he ordered the carpenters to set to work. The queen stood watching as both trees crashed to the ground. And a splinter flew upwards and entered her mouth, and she became pregnant.

Nine months later the queen gave birth to a fine and healthy son. Bata was reborn. Delighted with the new arrival, the king decreed that there should be celebrations throughout the whole land. He immediately appointed the boy Viceroy of Kush. Eventually he became Crown Prince, his father's sole heir. When the old king died the boy took his place on the throne of Egypt.

Then the new King of Egypt spoke. "Have all the high officials brought before me, so that I might tell them my history."

This was done. Next the faithless wife was then brought in, and Bata judged her before the whole court. She was found guilty, and condemned to meet the fate that the Seven Hathors had decreed for her, so many years before.

Next Anubis appeared before the court. To reward his loyalty, Bata appointed his brother Crown Prince. And when Bata eventually died after thirty years on the throne, it was Anubis who ruled in his stead.

Thus everything ended happily.

COMMENTARY ON
THE TWO BROTHERS

We have just one version of this remarkable tale, preserved on a
19th Dynasty papyrus (Papyrus D'Orbiney) by the scribe Ennana.
It starts out as a simple, almost believable account of two brothers
and a faithless woman; a story highly reminiscent of the Biblical
tale of Joseph and Potiphar's wife, which is also set in Egypt, and
not too different to the story of Webaoner which is included in the
Five Magical Tales. We expect something bad to happen to Anubis's
adulterous wife, and feel little sympathy for her when it does. But
the story then evolves into a complex fantasy involving travel,
gods, magic, another faithless woman and the resurrection of the
dead. What does this mean? Again the experts cannot agree.

It is no coincidence that both brothers have the names of gods.
Anubis is the jackal-headed funerary god, while Bata is a version of
Seth who is here heavily equated with the Canaanite storm god
Baal. Their story is partially set in Canaan, with Bata travelling from
his homeland to the Valley of the Cedar before returning home to
become King of Egypt. The Valley is a real place - the story of the
Battle of Kadesh tells us that Ramesses II, too, passed through the
Valley of the Cedar en route to war.

Some scholars have suggested that *The Two Brothers* should be
read, not as a simple folktale, but as the story of the descent of
Egypt's Ramesside kings from the divine entity Bata. The
Ramesside kings were not born to rule Egypt. They were a family
of successful generals who were adopted into the royal succession
by King Horemheb at the very beginning of the 19th Dynasty.
They hailed from the eastern Nile Delta and, as was the case with
all eastern Delta-dwellers, they are likely to have had blood-ties

with Egypt's eastern neighbours. A story "proving" their divine descent would have been regarded as excellent propaganda, particularly if it were written just before the coronation of Seti II, a time when the royal succession was in crisis. But others have argued that the story is a parable, telling the story of the sun's twenty-four hour journey across the sky.

The Ramesside kings had a very personal bond with Seth, the Red One, god of the eastern Delta site of Avaris. At least one of them - Ramesses II - had red hair. Red hair was as uncommon in Ancient Egypt as it is in Egypt today. Hair certainly plays an important role in this story, with Anubis's anonymous wife seemingly obsessed with her coiffure. As in our own culture, a clean, well-groomed head of hair - or indeed an elaborate wig - was considered attractive, but the neat plaits would be loosened and the wig would be removed for comfort when the woman lay down to sleep. Neat hair signified control and the presence of *maat*, whereas disordered hair indicated chaos. We find women in childbirth - the ultimate loss of control when the forces of life and death breach the security of the home - adopting wild-looking, archaic hairstyles. Those in mourning voluntarily tousled their hair, while women preparing to abandon themselves to wild lovemaking liberated their locks. Thus loose hair became inextricably linked with sexuality and lust and references to hair may occasionally be read as veiled references to eroticism. Prostitutes and female dancers certainly displayed the most elaborate of hairstyles, while poets rhapsodised over their lovers' tresses.

My heart thought how much I loved you when half of my hair was dressed. I came running to find you, and forgot about my hair. Now, if you let me plait, I shall be ready in a moment.

Hair, this time an exquisitely perfumed lock of hair, features again in the story of Bata's faithless and equally anonymous wife. This wife is an Egyptian Pandora. Made by the gods, she is infinitely tempting to the impotent Bata, but is herself fatally tempted by the luxuries of palace life. So seductive is the god-given scent of her hair that the King of Egypt is prepared to search the whole world for its owner. This part of the tale foreshadows the Cinderella-like story of Rhodophis, told by the classical author Strabo. In his much later tale, Rhodophis's sandal is stolen by an eagle, which flies to Memphis and drops the sandal into the King of Egypt's lap. Enchanted by its haunting perfume, the king orders an immediate search for the sandal's owner. Soon, in best fairytale tradition, the beautiful Rhodophis finds herself Queen of Egypt.

11

THE TALE OF TRUTH
AND FALSEHOOD

The lost beginning of this tale tells how Falsehood lent his brother Truth a fantastic dagger. Truth has failed to return the dagger, and so Falsehood has denounced him before the court of the gods. As we join the trial, Falsehood is about to describe his lost property, the like of which has never been seen before...

Falsehood spoke. "All the copper of Mount El went into its blade; all the timber in the Coptos wood was carved into its haft. Its sheath was the size of a rock-cut tomb; its belt was sewn from all the hides of the herd of Kal. And Truth has deliberately lost this most precious weapon. Let Truth now be brought before you, and let him be blinded in both eyes in punishment. Let him serve as my doorkeeper as a permanent reminder of his crime."

The court, judging Truth guilty, did as Falsehood asked. And the blinded Truth served as doorkeeper at the house of Falsehood.

One day Falsehood realised how truly good his brother was. And this realisation disturbed him - he could no longer feel comfortable with Truth living in his house. So Falsehood called Truth's servants to him. He ordered them to lead their master into the desert where he might be eaten by a wild lion with many hungry lionesses. The servants did as Falsehood commanded, and Truth was led into the desert. But Truth soon realised what was happening and pleaded with his servants to let him go. This they did, because they loved Truth and hated Falsehood. The servants returned home and lied to Falsehood, telling him that they had actually watched as a hungry lion devoured Truth.

Many days after this unhappy event, a fine lady came out of her house accompanied by her servants. She caught sight of Truth lying in the desert under a bush, and was impressed by his good looks and muscular physique. She desired him very much, so she sent her servants to bring him to her house so that he might become her doorkeeper. And that night blind Truth slept with the amorous lady, and the lady conceived a son.

The son born to the lady was a wonderful child; he was tall, healthy and strong, the son of a god. At school he excelled at writing and fighting, so that he surpassed even the boys who were older than him. But his school friends were jealous of his success, and they taunted him cruelly as schoolboys do: "Whose son are you? You don't have a father".

The boy was wounded by his friends' words. He went to his mother, and asked her to name his father. Much to his surprise she told him that his father was a member of her household.

"You see that blind man who guards our door. He is your father."

The boy was aghast, and rounded on his mother.

"You and all your family deserve to be fed to a crocodile, for treating my father with such disrespect."

He went straight away to his father, bringing him a comfortable chair and a footstool. He gave him good food to eat, and strong beer to drink, and then he questioned him.

"Tell me who blinded you, so that I might avenge you."

Truth told his son the whole, bitter story.

The son was determined to avenge his innocent father. He packed ten loaves of bread, a staff, a pair of sandals, a canteen of water and a sword. Then he fetched a beautiful ox, and drove it to his uncle's field. Here he spoke to the herdsman.

"Take my loaves, and my staff, my canteen, my sword and my sandals, for I do not need them. But please look after my beautiful ox until I return to collect him."

The herdsman was very happy with this arrangement, and gladly agreed to care for the ox for as long as the boy wanted. The beautiful ox was put amongst Falsehood's cattle, and thrived.

One day, while Falsehood was walking in the fields, he caught sight of the beautiful ox in the midst of his cattle. He ordered the herdsman to bring the beast to him, for he wanted to kill it and eat it. But the herdsman refused.

"It is not my ox sir, and so I cannot give it to you. That would not be right."

"Surely I can have this one ox, and you can give one of my cattle to its owner, in its place?"

And so it was done.

The young boy heard that his uncle had taken his ox and smiled. This was exactly what he had hoped would happen. Now he returned to the herdsman and demanded the return of his property. The herdsman, embarrassed, offered him the pick of Falsehood's cattle, but the boy would not be moved.

"None of these beasts is as big or as beautiful as my ox. My ox was as large as Egypt. If my ox stood on Amen's Isle its tail would brush the papyrus marshes while one horn rested on the eastern mountain, and one on the west."

The herdsman laughed at the boy's exaggeration.

"Don't be silly. There is no ox as large as the one you describe. It is impossible."

The boy seized hold of the herdsman, and dragged him before Falsehood. Then he summoned Falsehood to appear before the council of the gods.

The gods were not impressed with the boy's claim.

"What you have described is unbelievable. We have never seen an ox as large as the one you describe. It is quite impossible for an ox to be as large as Egypt."

But the boy persevered.

"So, you don't believe in my magnificent ox? Yet, not so long ago, you had absolutely no trouble believing that there could have been a dagger as large as the one this man once described to you, with all the copper of Mount El in its blade, all the timber in the Coptos wood in its haft? Its sheath the size of a rock-cut tomb, and its belt sewn from all the hides of the herd of Kal?"

Hearing this, the gods fell silent and started to listen to the young boy.

"Now the time has come for you to judge between Truth and Falsehood. For I am the son of Truth, and I have come to avenge my father for the wrong done to him."

Falsehood laughed, and lightly swore an oath before the gods. "Truth is dead - and anyway, he has no son. I swear before you all, that if you can find Truth still alive I shall be blinded in both eyes and become his doorkeeper."

Then the boy led the gods to his father, who was still sitting outside his mother's house, very much alive. So Falsehood received the most severe of punishments. He was beaten one hundred times, cut with five open wounds, and blinded in both eyes. And thus Falsehood became the doorkeeper in the house of Truth.

In this way the young boy avenged his father, and the quarrel between Truth and Falsehood was settled.

So everything ended happily.

COMMENTARY ON THE TALE OF TRUTH AND FALSEHOOD

This tale is preserved on the 19th Dynasty Papyrus Chester Beatty II. Unfortunately the beginning of the papyrus is entirely lost, and the opening section of the surviving text is riddled with gaps.

Like Anubis and Bata, Truth and Falsehood are brothers. But here the similarity ends, as theirs is a bitter relationship rotten with one-sided sibling rivalry more akin to the relationship between Osiris and his brother Seth. *The Tale of Truth and Falsehood* is an elaborate allegory dealing with the restoration of justice, or *maat*. It provides us with an interesting, if exaggerated, view of the Egyptian judicial system. In particular, it introduces us to the idea of compensation payments, and to the use of beatings and open wounds as physical punishments: one hundred blows plus five open wounds was the accepted penalty for perjury, which was a criminal rather than a civil offence. Blinding was not a common Egyptian punishment; as we have already noted, the Egyptians tended to favour amputations that would leave the criminal able to perform useful work for the state.

The name of the amorous lady, lover of Truth, is left deliberately blank in the text - linguists have speculated that she too might have had a personification, perhaps "Greed" or even "Lust" would suit her best.

Several real locations are specified in the story. The copper-rich Mount El is unknown, but Kal is a Nubian province, and Amen's Isle is not an island at all, but the Delta site of Tell el-Balamun.

FOUR TRUE STORIES

Every work of art is the fulfilment of a wish. Whether it be an excellent or a damnable work of art affects not at all that basic fact, but is merely a question of skill.

Terence Gray, '*And in the Tomb were Found...*' *Plays and Portraits of Old Egypt*, 1923

12

THE ADVENTURES OF HARKHUF

Carved to the right side of the entrance to the tomb:

The Royal Seal-Bearer, Sole Companion, Lector Priest and Chief of Scouts; the one who brings the produce of all foreign lands to the king and gives precious gifts to the queen; Governor of all the mountainlands of the south; the one who casts the shadow of dread of Horus over the foreign lands; the one who earns the praise of his lord; the one who is honoured by the god Sokar; Harkhuf speaks:

His Majesty King Merenre, my lord, sent me on my first mission to Yam, to explore and open up the trade route to that faraway country. And he sent my father, the Sole Companion and Lector Priest Iri, with me. I accomplished my mission in a mere seven months. I brought all kinds of beautiful and exotic goods back from Yam, and I earned the admiration and praise of my lord for my work.

The next time, His Majesty trusted me enough to send me on a mission alone. I travelled southwards out of Egypt along the Ivory Road, and I returned northwards via Mekher, Terers and Irtjetj (all of these are towns in Irtjet). I accomplished this mission in eight months, and I returned home bearing great quantities of precious things. Everyone was astonished, for no explorer had brought so many valuable goods back to Egypt before. On my way back I travelled through the region controlled by the chiefs of Setju and Irtjet, and explored those lands. No other envoy to Yam had managed to explore these faraway places as I did.

Then His Majesty sent me on a third mission to Yam. I travelled out from the province of This along the Oasis Road. I discovered that the ruler of Yam had set off for Tjemeh-land, with the intention of smiting the Tjemeh and driving them to the western corner of the sky. I followed the ruler of Yam to Tjemeh-land, and I pacified him and made him content so that he gave praise to all the gods for the King of Egypt.

Carved to the left side of the entrance to the tomb:

I sent a native courier to let His Majesty Merenre, my lord, know that I had gone to Tjemeh-land, following in the footsteps of the ruler of Yam. Then, when I had satisfied the ruler of Yam, I returned to the Nile Valley through the lands south of Irtjet and north of Setju. There I found the ruler of the triple alliance of Irtjet, Setju and Wawat. I arrived before him with three hundred donkeys loaded with all kinds of precious goods: incense, ebony, exotic oils and perfumes, panther skins, elephant tusks, throwing sticks and lots, lots more. Now, when the sole ruler of Irtjet, Setju and Wawat saw my impressive escort - the numerous troops provided by the grateful ruler of Yam plus, of course, the original army that had set off from Egypt with me - he too gave me an escort. He presented me with cattle and goats, and guided me along the mountain paths of Irtjet. This all happened because I had been more diligent in carrying out my duties than any other Companion and Chief of Scouts who had previously been sent to Yam.

As I was approaching the palace, the Sole Companion and Overseer of the Slaughter Houses, Khuni, was sent to meet me with ships filled with date wine, cakes, bread and beer...

Carved to the far right side of the entrance to the tomb:

A letter from King Neferkare Pepi II:
Day 15 of the third month of inundation, Year 2.
Written under the king's own seal.

The king writes to the Sole Companion, Lector Priest, and Chief of Scouts, Harkhuf. The dispatch that you sent to the palace, informing me that you and your army have returned in safety from Yam, has been received. In that dispatch you mention that you have brought with you many precious gifts; gifts that Hathor has provided for the spirit of King Neferkare Pepi, may he live forever. You specifically state that you have obtained a pygmy, one of the god's dancers, from the land of the horizon-dwellers. And you add that this pygmy is like the pygmy that the God's Seal Bearer Wer-Djed-Ba brought from the land of Punt during the reign of King Isesi. But, as you point out, your pygmy is the first of his kind to come to Egypt from Yam.

This is excellent news indeed. You really know how to please your lord. Truly, I think that you must spend all your waking hours working out how best to serve me. I will reward you and your family for many generations for this good deed. Everyone, when they hear of my generosity, will say: "Can anything ever equal the favours that were heaped on the Sole Companion Harkhuf, when he returned from Yam, as a reward for his irreproachable service to the king".

Make your way northwards to the palace, at once. Hurry, and bring with you the remarkable pygmy from the land of the horizon-dwellers, so that he might perform the dances of the god and delight my heart. Guard this pygmy with your life! When he is on board the ship, make sure that he is well supervised lest he fall into the water and drown. When he is in bed at night, have your loyal men care for him in his tent. Check on him at least ten times each and every night! For I long to see this remarkable pygmy more than

I long for all the precious gifts of Punt.

If the pygmy is still alive and well when you reach my palace, I will do great things for you. More, even, than was done for the God's Seal Bearer Wer-Djed-Ba during the reign of King Isesi, for so great is my desire to see the pygmy that you bring. Orders have been issued to ensure that supplies be provided from the storage depots and temple warehouses. No one will be exempted from this.

COMMENTARY ON
THE ADVENTURES OF HARKHUF

The Old Kingdom courtier Harkhuf carved his lengthy autobiography into the face of his rock-cut tomb for all men to see. In so doing, he followed a recently established precedent that saw Egypt's elite males - but never her royals - competing to display increasingly elaborate personal histories. These tales served two purposes. Designed to justify admittance to eternal life, they were also intended to impress literate passers-by, in the hope that they might be inspired to leave an offering to the spirit of the deceased. Factually accurate, but highly biased, they tell of the approved actions of faultless men, and emphasise links with the royal family while entirely overlooking the humdrum trivia and minor vices that lend texture to less-than-perfect lives. They are undeniably self-conscious and self-justificatory epitaphs carved by those who could afford to ensure that their deeds would live forever. Nevertheless, they often show great, if somewhat naive, charm. And at least two of these tales, the autobiography of Harkhuf at Aswan and the Abydos autobiography of his predecessor Weni, allow us a glimpse of life that would otherwise be completely lost. It is probably no coincidence that both these tales survived in southern provincial cemeteries, away from the capital city Memphis, and so away from any form of official censorship.

Both Weni and Harkhuf start their autobiographies by listing, and indeed in Harkhuf's case repeating, their ranks and titles. Some of these titles we can easily understand while others, such as the ubiquitous but enigmatic ranking title "Sole Companion", are more difficult, but invariably reflect the tomb owner's close relationship with the king. Harkhuf's favoured title "Chief of Scouts" is the designation usually given to expedition leaders.

The veteran politician Weni, "Count, Chamberlain, Warden of Nekhen, Mayor of Nekheb, etc, etc" gave many years of loyal and discreet service to King Teti and his son Pepi I. In one of the most tantalising snippets of gossip to survive unexplained from the Old Kingdom, he hints at dark goings-on in the 6th Dynasty royal harem:

> *When charges were brought in private in the royal harem against the queen "Great of Sceptre", His Majesty made me hear the case alone. No chief judge and vizier, no official was there, only me by myself... Never before had one like me heard a secret of the king's harem; but His Majesty allowed me hear it, because I was worthy in His Majesty's heart beyond any other official...*

Unfortunately, Weni is far too diplomatic to elaborate further, and his autobiography continues along more conventional lines with a dramatic account of a series of campaigns against the "Sand Dwellers" to the east of Egypt. When Pepi I was succeeded by his son Merenre, Weni became Governor of Upper Egypt. He took to his new role with vigorous enthusiasm, and tells us how he taxed his people, dug canals and quarried the precious stone that would eventually be used for Merenre's sarcophagus.

Harkhuf, too, served as Governor of Upper Egypt, first under Merenre and then, nine years later, under his young brother, Pepi II. Already Egypt was experiencing a foretaste of the economic and climatic problems that would eventually cause the collapse of central authority and end the Old Kingdom. But, although the royal pyramids had shrunk in size and the provincial governors had grown in power, superficially at least things continued very much as they had for centuries. Trade with the gold-rich yet ill-explored Nubia remained a matter of great importance. Nubia was at this time on friendly terms with her northern neighbour. But she too was changing and, of course, she was also experiencing the increasing aridity and desertification that were to devastate Egypt.

Harkhuf enjoyed at least four campaigns; three conducted during the reign of Merenre plus the one which is left to the imagination but which leads to his obtaining the coveted pygmy during the reign of Pepi II. These are linked together in a narrative that is heavy on atmosphere but disappointingly light on geographical detail. It is the inclusion of the letter about the pygmy, written by the young king, which really brings the text to life. Pygmies were much prized as sacred dancers; they are known to have danced before kings just as kings danced before gods, and they feature in the Pyramid Texts where their sacred dance forms part of the mortuary ritual. It is not surprising that Pepi, who is still a child ruling under his mother's guidance, can hardly control his impatience as he waits for Harkhuf to reach the palace. Harkhuf in turn is so delighted to receive a letter of praise from his king that he has it added in its entirety to his tomb façade.

Pepi's letter is specifically dated to "Day 15 of the third month of inundation, Year 2". As we have already seen, the Egyptian calendar had three official seasons; summer, inundation and winter. Years were dated by reference to the reign of the ruling king and, with each change of king, year-counting started again with Year 1. This made good sense to the Egyptians, who regarded each new reign as both a new beginning and a repetition of what had gone before. It did, however, mean that in order to understand their own history they were forced to keep long and accurate lists of kings.

Harkhuf's first expedition saw him travelling southwards to explore the trade route to Yam, a region or chiefdom of Upper Nubia. We cannot follow his travels on a map, because Egyptologists are still debating the exact location of Yam. But we do know that he was accompanied by, or more likely under the supervision of, his more experienced father Iri.

As all went well - exceptionally well, as Harkhuf himself tells us - on the first mission, he was permitted to make his next journey alone. Alone, of course, except for the military escort who always travelled with him. Setting off from an unspecified Egyptian town to an unspecified Nubian destination, he picked up the "Ivory Road" at Yebu (Elephantine). The Ivory Road was, as its name suggests, a desert trail used for the valuable trade in Nubian ivory. In eight months time, his mission accomplished, he returned home along the Nile Valley via the Lower Nubian region of Irtjet.

His third adventure saw Harkhuf travelling southwards from This (near Abydos) to Yam along the "Oasis Road" - a desert trail passing through the Western Desert and the Kharga Oasis. But this time the chief of Yam was absent - he had set off on his own campaign, to subdue the Tjemeh tribesmen who were threatening his lands. The "Tjemeh" are often translated as "Libyans", but here are better understood to be more generalised eastern Sahara nomads.

Acting on his own initiative Harkhuf followed the chief. We are not told why he decided to do this, but he surely cannot have expected to trade with the chief on the battlefield. He may perhaps have wanted to pacify him, or to offer official support for anyone who was prepared to fight the Tjemeh. Somehow he was able to satisfy the chief and earn his gratitude. Maybe the mere presence of an official Egyptian delegation, albeit a small one, was enough to cause the Tjemeh to back off. Harkhuf returned home through the allied lands of Irtjet, Setju and Wawat. This is his last recorded adventure although, as we can see from the dating of Pepi's letter, he enjoyed at least one further mission. Are we to assume that Harkhuf then abandoned his travels in favour of more sedate courtly activities, or was he able to retire on the bounty promised as his reward for bringing the pygmy to his king?

13

THE SIEGE OF MEGIDDO

Horus name: Strong Bull Arisen in Thebes
Two Ladies name: Enduring in Kingship like Re in Heaven
Golden Horus name: Mighty in Strength, Majestic in Appearance
The King of Upper and Lower Egypt, Lord of the Two Lands:
Menkheperre
The Son of Re: Tuthmosis, may he live forever.

His Majesty ordered that the great victories, granted to him by
the grace of the god Amen, be recorded within the temple
that he had built for his father Amen. The inscription was to record
every campaign, and to give details of the booty and tribute recovered from the foreign lands.

Day 25 of the fourth month of winter, Year 22:
His Majesty, mighty and valiant, marched past the fortress of Sile
en route to his first victory, to subdue and suppress those who
threatened Egypt's borders...

*Day 4 of the first month of summer, Year 23 (the day of the festival of the
king's coronation):*
His Majesty's army arrived at the town of Conquest-of-the-Ruler,
known to the Syrians as Gaza.

Day 5 of the first month of summer, Year 23:
His Majesty, mighty and valiant, marched from the town to overthrow the wretched enemy and extend the borders of Egypt. For his father, the great god Amen, had decreed that he should conquer all.

Day 16 of the first month of summer, Year 23:
His Majesty's army arrived at the town of Yehem and struck camp. His Majesty summoned his most experienced generals to a council of war, and briefed them on the situation.

"Our most hated enemy, the Prince of Kadesh, has arrived at the walled city of Megiddo, and there he remains. He has collected as his allies the rulers of all the lands that were once loyal to Egypt, plus rulers from as far afield as Naharin, Khor and Kedy. He has their horses, their troops and their people under his command. And, or so my spies tell me, he intends to sit firm and safe in Megiddo and wait to fight us there. Now, tell me what you think we should do."

The generals were troubled by this news. For, as they realised:

"The direct road that leads from Aruna to Megiddo passes over the mountain. It is a steep and narrow path, and our horses, soldiers and supplies will have to travel along it in single file. This will be dangerous. We know that the enemy is waiting for us somewhere along that road. Strung out, our troops will be highly vulnerable. The enemy will attack the unprotected vanguard, and the rearguard, not yet having passed the town of Aruna, will be unable to defend them. But there are two other, longer roads that also lead to Megiddo. One of these roads lies to the east, and arrives at Taanach. The other passes to the north of Djefti, and would bring us out on the north side of the city. Our valiant king should choose whichever of these two safer roads seems best to him. Do not make us march along the dangerous mountain pass."

The king received this advice in silence, then gave his judgement.

"As Re loves me, and as my father Amen loves me, as I feel the very breath of life and power in my nostrils, I am determined to travel along the difficult Aruna Road. Let those of you who wish to take the safer roads do so, but let those who wish to follow me make their choice now. For if we do not take the more dangerous road our enemies, those whom the great Re despises, will spread rumours of our cowardice."

Then the generals spoke to His Majesty. "May your father Amen, Lord of the Thrones of the Two Lands, protect you in all you do. We will follow Your Majesty wherever you go, just as a good servant always follows his master."

His Majesty stepped out of his tent, and addressed the assembled troops.

"Do not worry, men. Your valiant king will guide your steps as you take the narrow mountain path."

For the king had privately sworn an oath that he, personally, would lead his army along the dangerous road. Now the marching orders were announced, and every man and horse was allotted his place in the line. And at the head of the column marched the king.

Day 19 of the first month of summer, Year 23:
The King of Egypt awoke in his tent at the town of Aruna. His Majesty journeyed northwards, guided by his father Amen-Re, Lord of the Thrones of the Two Lands, who cleared a path before him. The god Horakhty emboldened the heart of the brave army, while Amen himself strengthened the king's own resolve.

The valiant king led his army along the straight and narrow pass, without meeting a single one of the enemy. For the enemy, cowards themselves, had assumed that the Egyptians would not be brave enough to take this perilous road, and were waiting instead along the wider roads that led to Taanach and the north side of Megiddo. So, while the rearguard of the Egyptian army was still waiting to march from Aruna, the vanguard had arrived safely in the Qina Valley. Soon the Valley was filled with Egyptian troops. And the king, rejoicing in his luck, called to his men to give thanks to the great god Amen who had guided their choice of path.

The generals now advised the king to wait in the valley until the rearguard had passed through the mountains. And, as this was a sensible plan, this is what the king did. He struck temporary camp in the valley and waited as his men came in single file along the path. It was noon before the last of the troops arrived in the valley.

His Majesty arrived at Megiddo, on the shore of the Qina River, at the seventh hour of the day. Here the soldiers pitched camp, the inspiring words of their generals ringing in their ears.

"Prepare yourselves for battle. Make sure that your weapons are sharp. For tomorrow we will have a glorious victory over our most wretched enemy."

So it was done. The officers were served a splendid meal while the troops received their rations. A guard was posted around the camp, with instructions to remain steadfast and vigilant at all times. And a message was brought to the royal tent:

"The whole region is safe, and so are the troops of the south and the north".

Day 21 of the first month of summer, Year 23 (the day of the feast of the new moon):
The king left his tent at dawn, and an order was given to the troops to make ready. The king stood proud in his golden chariot, covered in shining armour like the great warrior Montu, god of Thebes. His father Amen strengthened his sword arm. The southern flank of the Egyptian army was stationed on a hill south of the Qina River, the northern flank was stationed to the northwest of Megiddo, and His Majesty himself commanded the troops in the centre. Amen guaranteed the king's personal safety in the heat of battle, while Seth lent his strength to his limbs.

Riding at the head of his army, His Majesty overwhelmed the miserable enemy. Overcome by the glorious sight of the king and his brave men, the craven foes turned and ran hell-for-leather towards Megiddo, their faces ashen with fear. They abandoned their horses and their chariots on the battlefield, and ran to the safety of the city walls. But the city gates were already closed and would not now be opened lest the Egyptians gain entry. The fleeing enemy had to be hauled up the walls on ropes and sheets and even garments which the citizens inside lowered for them.

Now, if the Egyptian troops had obeyed their orders, and had not stopped to plunder the abandoned enemy camp, the battle would soon have been over. For the enemy, still being hauled up the city walls, were trembling with fear at the sight of His Majesty. But the fine horses, and the silver and gold chariots, made easy pickings, abandoned as they were on the battlefield. The Egyptians succumbed to temptation. They took everything that the enemy had left, even the tents. Then there was great rejoicing, and many hymns of praise were raised to Amen. For Amen had given his son victory that day. The soldiers cheered their king and celebrated his victory. They presented him with all the plunder taken from the battlefield: horses; gold and silver chariots; living prisoners and a pile of amputated hands.

His Majesty spoke to his troops.

"Listen well, my brave men. By the grace of Re, our enemy are walled up inside the city. Megiddo now holds a coalition of enemies drawn from many lands. When we capture the city, as we certainly will, we will indeed have conquered many lands. Remember this, and stand firm."

Orders went down to the section commanders to make sure that every man knew exactly what his duties were. Then the soldiers dug a large ditch around the walled city, surrounding it with a stockade of fresh timber stripped from the local fruit trees. The camp guards were warned to remain alert at all times. For no one was to be permitted to pass from the city beyond the encircling wall unless they were prepared to surrender to the Egyptians.

Everything that His Majesty did to the city of Megiddo and the wretched enemy within has been recorded in his campaign diary;

even today these details are recorded on a leather scroll in the temple of Amen.

Eventually the loathsome foreign princes left the city and came crawling on their bellies to kiss the ground before His Majesty. They begged for their lives, subdued by the strength of the king, and the might and power of the great god of Egypt, Amen. The wretched princes brought His Majesty great tribute. There were precious metals and stones; silver, gold, lapis lazuli, turquoise, and luxury goods; grain, wine and large and small cattle. One group of prisoners was appointed to carry the tribute back to Egypt. Then His Majesty chose new princes to lead every town...

List of the booty captured by His Majesty's troops at the city of Megiddo:

> Living prisoners - 340
> Hands - 83
> Horses - 2,041
> Foals - 191
> Stallions - 6
> Colts - unknown quantity
> Gold chariot - 1
> Gold chariot, property of the Prince of Megiddo - 1
> Chariots, property of the allied princes - 30
> Army chariots - 892
> Fine bronze coat of mail - 1
> Fine bronze coat of mail, property of the Prince of
>   Megiddo - 1
> Leather coats of mail - 200
> Bows - 502
> Wooden tent poles decorated in silver - 7
> Cattle - 387
> Cows - 1,929
> Goats - 2,000
> Sheep - 20,500

List of the booty carried off after the siege by the king, taken from the household goods of the enemy princes plus the property of the towns that had been loyal to them:

> Soldiers - 38
> Children - 84
> Guards - 5
> Male and female slaves and their children - 1,796
> Pardoned people who surrendered due to hunger - 103

In addition, sundry expensive bowls and vessels, knives, a statue, walking sticks, carrying chairs and furniture and a big heap of clothing.

The fields of the enemy were divided into plots and allocated to royal inspectors responsible for collecting their harvest.

COMMENTARY ON THE SIEGE OF MEGIDDO

The 18th Dynasty king Tuthmosis III spent the first twenty-two years of his reign in the shadow of his dominant co-ruler, the female pharaoh Hatshepsut. Immediately after her death he embarked on a series of campaigns designed to strengthen Egypt's eastern influence. In so doing he was following the example set by his grandfather, the respected general Tuthmosis I, who had marched his troops eastwards to the banks of the Euphrates River. At least sixteen seasonal campaigns would follow over the next twenty years. The details of these wars, the *Annals*, were recorded in daybooks by his scribes who travelled with the army to witness events first-hand. Later, when the empire was secure, they were copied onto the walls of the Karnak temple of Amen. This gives the writing an immediacy and believable realism - by Egyptian standards these are surprisingly modest compositions - which other, more formally composed texts, lack.

Like Harkhuf before him, Tuthmosis starts his story with his name. His is a lengthy one:

Horus name: Strong Bull Arisen in Thebes

Two Ladies name: Enduring in Kingship like Re in Heaven

Golden Horus name: Mighty in Strength, Majestic in Appearance

The King of Upper and Lower Egypt, Lord of the Two Lands: Menkheperre

The Son of Re: Tuthmosis

By the New Kingdom all kings of Egypt bore five names or titles that, it was hoped, reflected the ambitions and achievements of their forthcoming reign. The last of the five names, the nomen, was the personal name given to the king at birth. The preceding throne name was the name by which the king was known to his subjects. So, although we call this king Tuthmosis III, Tuthmosis being a classical version of the Egyptian name Djehuty-mes, "One Born of Thoth", his people would have known him as Menkheperre, "The Form of Re is Established". The throne name and the nomen were written in the oval cartouche that designated kingship.

Tuthmosis III, like all the Tuthmoside kings, was devoted to Amen, the "Hidden One", the great god of Thebes and father of kings. Amen was revered as the inspirational force who guided the fate of the victorious Egyptian army, and his Karnak temple complex became a permanent building site as successive kings competed to erect impressive monuments to their god. From our point of view Amen is a rather remote - dull, even - deity as he takes his "hidden-ness", or "inexplicableness" literally. No one knows the true name of the god Amen and he has little developed mythology, although he does have a wife, Mut, and a son, Khonsu, who have their own temples at Karnak.

Pre-New Kingdom temples had undoubtedly been impressive structures but they were built of mud-brick and, as most have long-since crumbled to dust, we have no opportunity of looking at the scenes that decorated their walls. The new custom of building temples in stone provided the gods with permanent homes, and the kings with a highly useful permanent propaganda tool. While the innermost temple walls were decorated with appropriate religious scenes, other walls were used to display scenes of victory and military might which emphasised the king's religious duty to preserve *maat* by destroying Egypt's enemies.

Our sudden ability to "read" temple walls can give the misleading impression that only in the New Kingdom did Egypt's kings show an interest in persecuting foreigners. This is far from the truth. Battles notoriously leave little archaeological evidence, but from Predynastic times onwards we have occasional images that show Egypt's kings smiting their traditional enemies; the Nubians (southerners), the Libyans (westerners) and the Asiatics (easterners). Nor should we fall into the trap of assuming that the battle-field was now Egypt's only point of contact with foreigners. International trade remained important throughout the New Kingdom. The Ulu Burun wreck, the well-preserved remains of a merchant ship that sank off the coast of Turkey during the reign of Seti I, confirms this. The cargo of the ship included goods from at least seven different cultures: copper from Cyprus; tin from either Turkey or Afghanistan; Baltic amber; Syrian ivory; Canaanite pottery; African ostrich eggs; Egyptian luxury goods.

Hatshepsut's reign had been one of peace, stability and international trade. Now, however, Egypt was threatened by developments outside her borders. Nubia, once Egypt's most dangerous foe, was temporarily resigned to her role as Egypt's most southerly province. She was governed by an Egyptian viceroy, and paid copious taxes into the Egyptian treasury. To the west the "Libyans", the diverse nomadic tribes of the eastern Sahara who had so vexed the Old Kingdom chief of Yam and the Middle Kingdom court of Amenemhat I, were keeping a low profile. But to the east Tuthmosis was faced with the task of controlling a collection of semi-independent fortified settlements with no real cultural or geographic unity and no particular reason to feel loyal to Egypt.

Whoever controlled the Levant and her ports would control the sea-based trade routes that underpinned the Mediterranean Bronze Age economy. And, as the wily Tuthmosis well recognised, a controlling interest in the Levant would effectively halt the expansion of Egypt's more ambitious eastern neighbours. Beyond the Euphrates the nation-state of Mitanni was gaining in power and influence in northern Mesopotamia. We have already visited a fictionalised version of Mitanni (Naharin) in *The Doomed Prince*. Of more immediate concern to Tuthmosis was the threat posed by Kadesh. The Prince of Kadesh, or so the spies reported, was busy spreading discontent amongst Egypt's former allies and a rebel coalition was even now camped outside the walled Canaanite city of

Megiddo (modern Tell el-Mutesellim, northern Israel).

Crossing the Sinai Peninsula the Egyptian army made for Gaza, a city loyal to Egypt since the start of the 18th Dynasty. From there they attacked and took Yehem, a fortified city occupied by a group of enemies headed by the Prince of Kadesh. Victory allowed the Egyptians to march eastwards across the Carmel mountain range to Megiddo. Here Tuthmosis decided to avoid the two long, relatively easy routes, leading the troops instead in single file along a narrow, winding, mountain road. This unexpectedly daring tactic allowed him to creep up on the enemy who were camped outside the city walls.

The battle was easily won but then, contrary to orders, the Egyptians paused to loot the abandoned enemy camps, and to cut hands from the corpses that littered the battlefield. Piles of hands and penises made the counting of the dead easy, and grizzly heaps of body parts are often included in the carved battle scenes that decorate temple walls. Unfortunately, while the Egyptian army was distracted, the city gates were shut. This was very irritating, but by no means a disaster. Tuthmosis knew that all he had to do was to sit tight and wait: with access to water and food, he had the upper hand. After seven long months hungry Megiddo surrendered and Tuthmosis gathered his rewards. With the collapse of the coalition he now had full control of Palestine and most of Syria. The Egyptian empire had been born. Over a thousand years later, when the writer of the Book of Revelation (16:16) wrote of the last great battle, he would set it here, at Megiddo:

And he gathered them together in a place called in the Hebrew tongue Armageddon.

Egypt would never attempt to absorb her eastern territories as she had Nubia. There would be no eastern viceroy, and the region would remain divided into a series of city-states whose kings and chiefs were allowed to retain their hereditary titles. These local rulers were, however, expected to confirm their allegiance to Egypt by supplying plentiful "gifts" of tribute that would be used to finance Egypt's extensive building programme. Their young children were sent as unofficial hostages to Egypt where they entered either the royal school or the royal harem. Sons, suitably brainwashed in the Egyptian way of thought, might eventually be allowed home to rule. Their sisters remained in Egypt.

14

THE BATTLE OF KADESH

VERSION ONE: THE BULLETIN

Day 9 of the third month of summer, Year 5: under the majesty of Re-Horakhty; the Strong Bull Beloved of Maat; the King of Upper and Lower Egypt; Usermaatre Setepenre; the Son of Re; Ramesses, Beloved of Amen; may he be given eternal life.

Ramesses was in Palestine, on his second victorious campaign. He awoke, full of vigour and health, in his tent in the hill country to the south of Kadesh. That morning His Majesty appeared glorious like the rising of Re. His Majesty marched northwards, and arrived in the region to the south of the town known as Shabtuna.

Here the glorious Egyptian army stumbled across two nomads. The two vagrants were dragged before His Majesty, and spoke to him with great sincerity.

"Our brothers, who are allies of the vile Hittite foe, have sent us to tell you that we intend to switch our allegiance and serve the noble King of Egypt instead."

The king smiled, and then questioned the men closely.

"Where are they then, these important brothers who have sent you with this message for me?"

"They remain with the vile ruler of the Hittites. For the enemy is cowering many miles away in the land of Khaleb, to the north of

Tunip. They are too frightened to come closer. When he heard that the King of Egypt had arrived, the leader of the Hittites lost all his courage and would not allow his army to move south."

But the two nomads who appeared to speak so frankly to the King of Egypt were devious liars. They were secret agents, sent by the vile ruler of the Hittites to find the King of Egypt and lull him into a false sense of security. The awful truth was, the Hittite ruler had already arrived at Kadesh, accompanied by his infantry and his chariots. With him were the chiefs of all his vassal states and their foot soldiers and chariots. Even as the spies lied to the king, the enemy was standing well equipped and well prepared behind the old city of Kadesh. And His Majesty had absolutely no idea that they were there.

When the two nomads had finished speaking they were released. His Majesty marched his division northwards with a light heart. He pitched camp northwest of Kadesh, and sat at peace on his throne of finest gold.

Then a soldier came into the king's presence, dragging with him two more "nomads" found skulking round the camp. To capture two nomads might be seen as good luck - to capture two more so soon afterwards was worrying. With mounting dread His Majesty questioned the prisoners.

"Who exactly are you? I want the truth."

"We are agents loyal to the noble King of Hatti. He has sent us to find you and spy on you."

"Where is he then, this vile enemy from Hatti? I understand that he is cowering many miles away in the land of Khaleb, to the north of Tunip."

"No sire, you are very wrong. The King of Hatti has already arrived at Kadesh, together with many who have rallied to his cause. His allies include the lands of Dardany, Naharin, Keshkesh, Masa, Pidasa, Karkisha, Luka, Carchemish, Arzawa, Ugarit, Irun, Inesa, Mushanet, Kadesh, Khaleb and, last but not least, the entire land of Kedy. They are armed with both infantry and chariots, and their weapons of war have been prepared. They are more numerous that the grains of sand on the shore. They stand equipped and ready for battle behind the old city of Kadesh."

Hearing these words, Ramesses shouted for his generals so that they too might learn the truth. Then, his heart dark with anger, His Majesty addressed his officers.

"We now find ourselves in a very difficult situation. For days my soldiers have been telling me that the vile enemy is cowering many miles away - that the ruler of the Hittites ran away in fear of my might. But now, just this very minute, by cunning questioning I have learned that he is, in fact, near by! And he is not alone. He has a mighty army with him and his men and horses are as numerous as the grains of sand on the seashore. Apparently, they are all hidden behind the old city of Kadesh. And yet not one of my officers, not one of my scouts or spies, was able to detect so large an army so close by."

Ashamed, the generals hung their heads and nodded their agreement. Then, with a bit of quick thinking, they laid the blame for the debacle fairly and squarely on their men.

"It is criminal, what the scouts and spies have done to you, Your Majesty. Incredibly, unbelievably, they have failed to notice a huge enemy army lurking close by our camp."

The vizier was dispatched with all speed to summon the remainder of the divided army. Then, as Ramesses was still closeted with his generals, the ruler of the Hittites struck with his infantry and his chariots and his many allies. Crossing the ford to the south of Kadesh the enemy charged into the Egyptians as they marched along, unaware of their danger. The Egyptian soldiers, caught off guard, fled before the enemy leading them northwards, directly into the royal camp. Soon the troops of the vile enemy surrounded the loyal Egyptian soldiers who guarded His Majesty.

When the king caught sight of the enemy he was stirred with the violent rage of his father Montu. Seizing his weapons and donning his armour, he became like Seth in the moment of his power. He mounted his great horse Victory-in-Thebes, and rushed off into the thick of battle. His Majesty was so brave and so determined, that none could stand before him. Around him the ground blazed with flames. He burned all the countries with his frenzied stare. His eyes glittered with a white-hot rage, and his awesome power scorched the enemy. His Majesty was indifferent to the miserable foe - he regarded the enemy as mere chaff, to be swept aside. He charged into the Hittites and their allies. His Majesty slayed the entire Hittite force, plus their allies. Their foot soldiers and their chariots piled up, one on top of another, and His Majesty slaughtered them where they fell. They dropped before his horses and His Majesty killed them.

My Majesty caused the forces of the Hittite foe to fall into the River Orontes, one on top of the other just as crocodiles fall into water. I pounced on them with the fury of a wild beast. When I attacked the allied soldiers I was alone; my infantry and my charioteers had deserted me. None of them stood with me, not one of them even looked back towards me. On my own life, as Re loves me and as my father Atum favours me, I swear that I am telling the truth.

VERSION TWO: THE POEM

His Majesty was a young and vigorous lord without an equal in the whole world. His arms were powerful and his heart was brave. His strength was like Montu when roused, while his beauty was like Atum who shines in the sky. He was victorious over all the foreign lands; a cunning strategist and a strong wall who inspired his troops and shielded them on the field of battle. He was a bowman of unparalleled skill, capable of defeating a multitude. His Majesty never hesitated, but charged straight into the massed enemy, trusting his strength and his brave heart just as the flame does not hesitate but consumes all in its path. A thousand men could not halt him: a hundred thousand fell before his fierce gaze.

He is the lord of fear, whose reputation has spread through all the lands. His is awesome and glorious, just as Seth is glorious on his mountain. He strikes terror into the dark hearts of foreigners just as the wild lion brings terror to a valley full of tame goats. He charges forth with valour, and he returns in triumph. He looks men straight in the eye, and he has no need to boast. He is upright in his conduct and is an excellent strategist; his first instinct is always right. In the thick of battle he rescues his soldiers and fights alongside his charioteers. He returns home with his army intact, having saved his soldiers from danger with a heart as firm as a mountain of copper. He is the King of Upper and Lower Egypt Usermaatre Setepenre; the Son of Re; Ramesses, Beloved of Amen; may he be granted eternal life like Re.

His Majesty had prepared a mighty army of infantry, charioteers and the Sherden mercenaries whom he had captured at an earlier battle. They had been supplied with their provisions and had received their battle orders. Now, on day nine of the second month of summer, Year 5, he set off northwards with his infantry and his chariots. His Majesty passed the fortress of Sile, appearing glorious like Montu to all who saw him. All the foreign lands trembled before His Majesty, for they were deeply frightened of his might. His Majesty's splendid army travelled along the narrow foreign paths with full authority, just as they might have travelled along Egyptian roads.

Eventually His Majesty reached Ramesses-Meramun, a town in the Valley of the Cedar. Still he continued northwards until he gained the hill country of Kadesh. He forded the river at the head of the Amen division, and soon stood before the city.

Now the vile ruler of Hatti had gathered together all the foreign lands as far as the end of the sea. The entire land of Hatti had come, and the lands of Naharin, Arzawa, Dardany, Keshkesh, Masa, Pidasa, Irun, Karkisha, Luka, Kizzuwadna, Carchemish, Ugarit and Kedy. The lands of Nuges were with him, as were the lands of Mushanet and Kadesh. He had not exempted a single country from his service, and their chiefs were with him. Together with their infantry and chariotry they made a greater number than had ever been seen. They covered the mountains and filled the valleys and were as numerous as locusts in a field. The ruler of Hatti had stripped his country of its wealth and its silver, and given it to his allies as a bribe so that they would support his cause.

The vile enemy from Hatti and his many foreign allies waited, hidden and ready for battle, to the northeast of Kadesh. Meanwhile His Majesty was alone and unprepared. The division of Amen, the best of his troops, marched with him. Behind them, the Re division was crossing the river close by the town of Shabtuna. The Ptah division was even further behind, to the south of the town of Ironama, while the Seth division was still marching on the open road. But the vile chief of the Hittites stood in the midst of his assembled armies and did not move. For, even though he had summoned so many men and horses that his troops resembled the grains of sand on the shore (there were three men to a chariot, each equipped with weapons), he was frightened of the King of Egypt.

The massed enemy remained hidden like cowards behind the town of Kadesh.

Then, suddenly, the enemy came from the south of Kadesh to ambush the Re division as they marched along, ignorant of their danger. Taken by surprise, the Re division weakened and fled before the enemy. This happened when His Majesty was stationed far away to the north of Kadesh, on the west bank of the Orontes. Messengers brought the terrible news to His Majesty. He rose up in anger like his father Montu. He donned his armour, seized his weapons, and grew terrible like Baal in the hour of battle. The great horse that bore His Majesty was Victory-in-Thebes, a horse of the royal stable.

His Majesty rode forth in his chariot and, all alone, charged the massed enemy from Hatti. Then, looking around, he saw that he was cut off from his troops and surrounded by 2,500 enemy chariots.

There was no officer with me, no charioteer, no soldier and no shield bearer. My infantry and my chariotry had fled before the enemy and not one stood firm to fight. I prayed aloud.

"What is happening, O father Amen? Is it right for a father to turn his back on his son? Are you determined to ignore my plight? This cannot be. Amen, Lord of Egypt, is surely too great to allow foreigners to step on his path.

"What do these wretched, godless Asiatics mean to you, Amen? I have built you many monuments, and filled your temples with treasure. I dedicated my Mansion-of-Millions-of-Years to you, and gave you all my wealth as endowments. I gave you the lands that you needed to support your altars. I sacrificed ten thousand cattle and burned many kinds of sweet herbs before you. I built magnificent gateways to you, and erected their flagpoles myself. I brought you seaworthy ships, and obelisks from Yebu.

"Will people now say 'There is little to be gained by trusting the will of Amen?' I am counting on you. Do the right thing by me, and

I will serve you with a loving heart for the rest of my life.

"I call upon you, my father Amen. I am in the midst of a host of hostile strangers. I am entirely alone; there is no one with me. My troops have run away, and not one of my charioteers is prepared to defend me. I shout for help, but they do not come. Yet I know that Amen will help me more than a million troops, more than a hundred thousand charioteers, more than ten thousand brothers and sons. The deeds of mortals are as nothing - Amen is a far greater help than they could ever be."

Although I prayed in a distant land my prayer was heard in far-away Thebes. Amen listened when I called to him; he gave me his hand and I rejoiced. He spoke to me clearly, as if he were nearby.

"Go forward my son, for I am with you. Your father is with you and is guiding your hand. I will triumph over a hundred thousand men, for I am the lord of victory and I will reward your valour."

Suddenly my heart grew strong and my breast swelled with joy. I knew that I was invincible and unstoppable. I had become the great god Montu. I appeared before the enemy like Seth in his moment. The enemy chariots scattered before my horses. Not one of them could stand and fight. Their hearts quaked with fear when they saw me and their arms went limp so they could not shoot. They did not have the heart to hold their spears. I made them plunge into the river just as crocodiles plunge into the water. They fell on their faces, one on top of another. I slaughtered them at my will. They did not look back, they did not turn around. Those who fell down did not rise.

The vile ruler of Hatti stood amongst his troops and chariots watching me fight, all alone, without my soldiers and my chariots. He stood quaking with fear, and was too scared to advance to meet me. He sent instead many chiefs, each armed with chariots and weapons of war. The allies of Hatti all came together; a hundred thousand chariots drove straight into the fire of battle. For my part I charged towards them like Montu in all his glory. In just one moment they felt the might of my hand. I slaughtered a great number and they dropped dead at my feet.

One managed to call out to the others. "Surely this is no human who is amongst us. It is Seth Great-of-Strength, Baal in person. His actions are not the deeds of mortal man. They are the deeds of one who can fight a hundred thousand unaided. Run as fast as you can! Flee before him so that you might live to see another day! For anyone who attempts to approach this being finds that his hands, indeed all his limbs, grow weak and limp. They cannot hold either bow or spear when they see him running towards them."

And all the while I hunted them down like wild beasts, slaughtering them without pause.

I raised my voice to call to my army.

"Be brave, my troops. Look, I am victorious, all alone! For Amen is my helper, and his hand is guiding me.

"What cowards you are, my charioteers - all of you have betrayed my trust. Did I not earn your allegiance by my deeds back home? Did I not select you for promotion? Did I not maintain *maat*? Whenever you petitioned me, I agreed to your requests. I allowed you to live in your villages without performing your duties, because I believed that you would repay my loyalty by answering when I summoned you to battle. But now you have all been proved cowards, and not one of you has stood fast by my side. As the spirit of my father Amen endures, I wish that I were back in Egypt like my fathers who never saw the Asiatics and never fought against them. Not one of you will be able to speak with pride of his service when he has returned home. The crimes of my soldiers and my charioteers are almost too dark to tell."

Fortunately, in that dark hour when I had no soldiers and no chariots, Amen lent me his strength. He allowed me to triumph over the foreign lands. I was completely alone. There was no captain to support me, no charioteer, infantryman or officer to help. Now the lands that have witnessed my valiant deeds will spread my fame to the limits of the known world. Those who escaped my arm, and turned back to see, they will speak of this...

When Menena my shield bearer saw that I was surrounded by a great number of enemy chariots, he too became weak and faint hearted. A great fear flooded his limbs, and he spoke to me.

"Great lord, strong ruler, saviour of Egypt. We stand alone in the carnage of battle, abandoned by our soldiers and our chariotry. Why do you stand firm to protect these worthless men? Let us, too, flee to safety. Save us, Usermaatre Setepenre."

But I replied to him.

"Stand firm and steady your heart, my shield bearer. I will charge the enemy just as the falcon pounces on her prey. I will slaughter them, butcher them, and fling their carcasses to the ground. Why do you fear these weaklings? They mean nothing to me."

Then I galloped forward and charged into the midst of the foe. Six times I charged them and I slaughtered them without pause...

My soldiers and my charioteers saw that I was strong-armed like Montu in his glory. They saw that my father Amen was with me, trampling the foreigners into chaff beneath my feet, and they came creeping back in shame one by one, entering the camp by night. They found the enemy lying dead in pools of congealing blood. For I had wrought havoc on the plain of Kadesh and the sheer number of bodies now made it difficult to walk. Seeing this, my soldiers came to honour me, their faces bright at the sight of my deeds. My captains and my charioteers paid tribute to my strong arm, and praised my name out loud.

"Hail to you, great warrior with the strongest of hearts. You have saved your foot soldiers and your charioteers. You are truly the son of Amen, and you act with his arms. Your great strength has felled the Hittites. You are the perfect warrior, a fighter beyond compare. You are great-hearted, foremost amongst kings, and the massed ranks of the enemy mean nothing to you. Protector of Egypt, scourge of the foreigner, you have broken the back of the Hittites forever."

Then I in turn spoke to my foot soldiers and my charioteers.

"And what about you, my gallant ones, you who fled the field of battle? A man should be brave, so that he may be acclaimed as a hero when he returns home from the war. A reputation earned on the battlefield is a good reputation indeed. The valiant man is always respected.

"Have I ever failed you, that you would consider leaving me alone in the midst of a battle? You are lucky to be still alive, you who ran away leaving me all alone. Did you not know, deep in your hearts, that I am your wall of iron? What will men say when they hear what you have done? That you left me alone, and that no chief, charioteer or soldier came to my aid while I was fighting? That I crushed the soldiers of a million lands by myself?

"My two great horses, Victory-in-Thebes and Mut-is-Content, gave me their unstinting support when I was alone, fighting the representatives of many lands. From this time on, whenever I am at the palace, they will feed in my presence as a reward for their support.

The charioteer Menena, my loyal shield bearer, and my household butlers also remained at my side to witness my victory. Only when I had killed a hundred thousand men did I pause in my quest for triumph."

As dawn broke I marshalled my troops for victory. I was ready to fight like an eager bull. Once again I assumed the role of Montu, and took up my weapons of victory. I charged into their ranks just as the falcon pounces on her prey. The snake on my brow breathed her fiery breath into the enemy's faces, and I was like Re when he rises at morn. My flames scorched the rebels, and again they called out to each other in fear.

"Take care, don't go near him! Sekhmet the Terrible is helping him! She is with him on his horse, and her hand guides his. Anyone foolish enough to approach him will be burned by her breath."

Hearing these words they retreated and bowed before me. My Majesty overcame the enemy. I slaughtered them without pity. They fell before my horses and lay in heaps saturated with their own red blood.

Then the vile chief of the Hittites wrote to me in the most flattering of terms:

"Re-Horakhty; Strong bull beloved of Maat; King who protects his army; Made mighty by his strong arm; Rampart to his soldiers in battle; King of Upper and Lower Egypt Usermaatre Setepenre; the Son of Re; Lord of Strength; Ramesses, Beloved of Amen; may he be given eternal life.

"Your humble servant writes to confirm that you are indeed the son of Re. Re has given all the lands in the world to you, and Egypt and Hatti are merely the servants under your feet. Do not overwhelm us. For you are indeed mighty and your strength lies heavy on the land of the Hittites. It is not good that you should turn your pitiless face towards your servants and kill them. Yesterday you killed a hundred thousand, and today you came back and killed yet more. Now is the time to show mercy, O victorious king. Peace is better than war. Allow us the chance of life!"

I relented, being magnanimous like Montu in his moment of victory. I summoned the generals of my infantry and the captains of the chariots and all my senior officers, and I read to them the words of the vile chief of the Hittites. With one voice, they cried aloud: "Peace is an excellent thing, O sovereign lord. There is no shame in following the path of peace when you are the victor."

Hearing this, I decided to agree to peace.

Travelling under the protection of the gods and goddesses of Egypt, His Majesty and his army returned home in peace. He had crushed the foreign lands. His personal bravery had protected his army, and all the foreign lands now praised his fair face.

COMMENTARY ON
THE BATTLE OF KADESH

We know that Tuthmosis III was a great soldier because his military record speaks for itself. We know that Ramesses II, "The Great", was a valiant and highly successful soldier because he tells us so, time and time again. Unfortunately, in spite of his efficient propaganda machine, his military record does not quite live up to his extravagant claims. One thing seems certain, though. The Battle of Kadesh was an event of huge importance to Ramesses. His telling of the tale, biased though it undoubtedly is, attempts to convey some of the real horror that he felt on that faraway battlefield.

As a young man Ramesses had waged a series of low-key campaigns against Egypt's traditional enemies, the Nubians to the south and the Libyans to the west, and he also saw off the Sherden pirates who were threatening Egypt's Mediterranean coast. But like Tuthmosis a century and a half before him, Ramesses looked to the east for personal glory. In Canaan and Syria he repeatedly matched his professional army against individual city-states. Lengthy siege followed lengthy siege. Ramesses invariably won the individual battles only to find, as he marched away from the sacked townships, that things soon reverted back to normal and he was forced to take action all over again.

At Kadesh-on-the-Orontes (modern Tell Neby Mend), a fortified Syrian city, Ramesses fought his most famous battle. This was a matter of family honour for as a young boy Ramesses had stood at his father's side as Seti I tried to take the city. Seti had been forced to accept an ignominious peace treaty; essentially he had lost. Then, as now, the enemy was a mighty coalition of local rulers led by the Hittites, "the vile enemy from Hatti", a powerful and ambitious foe based on the central Anatolian plateau in modern Turkey.

Whether or not Ramesses won this battle is a matter of interpretation. Ramesses certainly believed that he did, and the story of his triumph was preserved many times in prose (*The Bulletin*; a brief and largely factual account; seven surviving copies), in verse (*The Poem*; longer and more prone to flights of fantasy; eight surviving copies) and in carved relief with brief explanatory captions. At Karnak the tale filled the south exterior wall of the hypostyle hall; at the nearby Luxor Temple it was told three times; across the river at the Ramesseum (Ramesses's mortuary temple) it appeared twice in the forecourts; away from Thebes the residents of Abu Simbel and Derr (Nubia) and Abydos could each enjoy their own version. These versions have survived because their temple walls have survived. We might reasonably expect that Ramesses also carved his story into the walls of his now-vanished northern temples so that the citizens of Pi-Ramesses and Memphis could read of their king's triumph. We do have three additional papyrus versions of the story plus a cuneiform letter written from Ramesses to Hattusilis III.

As the hieroglyphic writing does not make the divisions into lines obvious, experts have argued for many years whether *The Poem* was truly intended to be read as metrical verse. Here I have followed the usual convention of rendering this account prose style; the introduction and ending of *The Poem* were, in any case, written as straight narrative prose.

The Bulletin, *The Poem* and the accompanying illustrations vary slightly in content, but tell essentially the same story. The narrative of both *The Bulletin* and *The Poem* switches between the third person and the first person, a dramatic device employed by New Kingdom authors to add an immediacy and authenticity to their work. Unfortunately, it is at exactly the point where the king takes over the telling that the tale departs from the believable and enters the realm of exaggerated fiction. Ramesses undoubtedly had a life-changing experience on the battlefield. He may even have persuaded his people that he was able to fight and subdue an entire army single-handed, but today we tend to take such claims with a rather large pinch of salt.

Our story starts in Year 5, but campaigning had already started in the summer of Year 4, when Ramesses marched along the coast to confirm Egypt's hold over Canaan and the Levantine ports. The strategically important region of Amurru, hitherto loyal to the Hittites, was "persuaded" to change allegiance and became home to a division of elite Egyptian soldiers. Ramesses made no secret of his intention to take Kadesh, and the ruler of Amurru was allowed to write to the Hittite king, Muwatallis, telling him exactly what had happened. Muwatallis, enraged, swore a sacred oath to re-gain his lost lands. He assembled a magnificent army of 2,500 chariots and 37,000 soldiers including infantrymen, mercenaries and some of the pirates whom Ramesses had expelled from the Delta. The remaining pirates, "the Sherden", were already fighting as mercenaries alongside the Egyptian army. They may be identified, in the reliefs, by their un-Egyptian round shields and curious bobble-topped helmets.

Next spring campaigning started in earnest. The Egyptian army, 20,000 strong, and therefore half the size of the Hittite forces, was sub-divided into four divisions, each marching under the standard of a protective god: Amen (Theban soldiers), Re (Heliopolis), Ptah (Memphis) and Seth (northeast Delta). The troops, horses and chariots were accompanied by pack animals and carts filled with provisions including such apparent essentials as Ramesses's golden throne, and these were followed in turn by an eclectic assortment of camp followers including high-ranking politicians and members of the royal family who often accompanied their lord and master to war. This lengthy convoy took a month to pass through Canaan and south Syria and, making use of the Bekaa Valley, to approach Kadesh from the south. Meanwhile an elite force marched along the coastal route - they would join forces with the Egyptians already stationed in Syria and attack Kadesh from the north.

So far so good. But safely camped ten miles to the south of

Kadesh, the impulsive Ramesses made a potentially fatal error of judgement. Two enemy spies managed to convince him that the Hittites were still 120 miles away at Khaleb (Aleppo). Throwing all caution to the wind he decided to head straight for Kadesh. With luck, he could launch a surprise attack and take the city before the Hittites arrived. The army split into its four divisions, and the Amen division, led by Ramesses, crossed the river and marched to make camp on the high ground to the northwest of Kadesh. The Re division followed close behind, then Ptah and finally Seth.

Only when the Egyptian army was spread across both sides of the river, did the capture and forced confession of two further Hittite spies (the illustrations accompanying the text show the spies being beaten) make the folly of this plan clear. Muwatallis had already reached Kadesh and was poised for an immediate ambush. The vizier rode post haste to summon the missing divisions, and the vulnerable royal family retreated to a position of safety. Now there was only time for a brief council of war; a highly acrimonious and somewhat infantile meeting which saw Ramesses blaming his generals, and the generals blaming their own men for the disaster. Suddenly the Hittites launched a fierce attack on the Re division.

The soldiers of Re, caught completely off guard, fled northwards, leading the enemy straight to the Egyptian camp. Now the soldiers of the Amen division panicked and fled. Ramesses found himself alone, surrounded by the enemy. Only the great god Amen, and his loyal shield bearer Menena, could help him now.

What really happened next? Ramesses tells us that he, single-handed but with the help of the god Amen, fought off the entire Hittite army. There has to be more to it than that. Muwatallis too had made a mistake. Over-confident of victory, he had not committed his full infantry to the ambush, and the bulk of the Hittite army, including the infantry, still stood on the east bank of the Orontes. The timely arrival of the Egyptian elite troops from Amurru - who are not specifically mentioned in the texts but whose arrival can be seen in one of the illustrations - came as an unpleasant shock. Reinforced, Ramesses was able to push back the Hittites who fled, swimming (and in some cases drowning in) the Orontes, to their colleagues. Then the Ptah division arrived, led by the valiant vizier, and the deserters of Re and Amen returned to stand by their king. By the time the Seth division arrived, the battle was over.

We are not sure what happened the next morning, as the texts are somewhat cryptic, but it is clear that more blood was spilt, and that once again the ground was littered with heaps of bodies. Did battle briefly resume? Or did Ramesses take the opportunity to punish his own cowardly troops for their desertion?

The Hittites and the Egyptians had reached stalemate; they sat in their respective camps, glowering at each other across the Orontes. Both had had a nasty fright. Both had realised, for perhaps the first time, that they might actually lose a battle.

Eventually, or so the Egyptian records tell us, the Hittite king sent a grovelling letter pleading for peace. A truce was agreed although Ramesses, claiming an Egyptian victory, refused to sign a formal treaty with his vanquished enemy. Perhaps he had a faint hope that he might one day return to claim his victory. The Hittite records, recovered from their capital at Hattusas (the Turkish site of Bogazkoy), tell a very different tale which ends with a humiliated Ramesses forced into ignominious retreat. The known facts tend to support this Hittite version of events. Ramesses's departure allowed the Hittites to regain control of Amurru. They then pushed south through the Bekaa Valley to expand their sphere of influence and secure the Egyptian territory of Upi. Meanwhile Ramesses was forced to launch a series of campaigns to restore his hold over Canaan and Syria.

Those who like a happy ending will be glad to learn that, sixteen years later, Egypt and Hatti did sign a peace treaty. And eventually, in Year 35, the twice-widowed Ramesses took a beautiful Hittite princess as a bride. Maathorneferure bore Ramesses a daughter before dying young. Ramesses grieved, then ten years after his first Hittite marriage, married a second Hittite princess.

15

THE VOYAGE OF WENAMEN

On day 16 of the second month of summer, Year 5, Wenamen, Elder of the Portal of the Temple of Amen, set off on his travels. His mission was to acquire the timber needed for the construction of the magnificent riverboat of Amen-Re. The name of the god's riverboat was Amen-Mighty-of-Prow.

I arrived in Tanis, home to Smendes and his wife Tantamen. I handed over the letter from Amen-Re, King of the Gods, and it was read out to them. The royal couple graciously agreed to do as the god had asked. I stayed in Tanis until the fourth month of summer. Then Smendes and Tantamen waved me off in the care of the Syrian ship's captain Mengebet. On the first day of the first month of the inundation I sailed down to the great Syrian Sea.

Eventually I reached Dor, a Tjeker port. On hearing of my arrival Beder, Prince of Dor, sent me fifty loaves, an amphora of wine and an ox haunch.

That night a very bad thing happened. A member of my ship's crew ran away, taking with him a gold vessel worth 5 *deben*, four silver jars worth 20 *deben*, and a bag holding 11 *deben* of silver. In total he stole 5 *deben* worth of gold and 31 *deben* worth of silver from me.

The next morning, as soon as I learned the bad news, I visited the prince. I had to speak quite forcefully to him.

"I have just been robbed in your harbour. You are the prince of this land; you are responsible for its justice. You must find my missing money! For it is not really my money. It belongs to Amen-Re, King of the Gods. It belongs to Smendes, and to Herihor my lord and to the other nobles of Egypt. It belongs to you; it belongs to Weret; it belongs to Mekmer; last but not least, it belongs to Tjeker-Baal, Prince of Byblos."

The Prince of Dor was taken aback by my words.

"You must be joking! I don't understand your reasoning at all. If a thief from my land had crept down to your ship and stolen your goods, then of course I would compensate you from my own treasury until the thief had been caught and your property restored. But the thief who robbed you came from your ship. He has to be your responsibility. Nevertheless, stay here for a few days, so that I may search for him and find your property for you."

I spent a fruitless nine days moored in his harbour. Then I returned to the prince. "Look here, you have failed to find the man who stole my property. Let me continue my journey."

Here the text is fragmented. It seems that the Prince of Dor attempts to persuade Wenamen to wait, but our hero is anxious to be on his way. He sails to the port of Byblos. There, just outside the harbour, perhaps following Beder's advice, he takes the law into his own hands. He confiscates 30 deben of silver from a ship belonging to the Tjeker. He tells the owners that their property will be returned only when his own goods are found. Not surprisingly, this act of piracy incenses the Tjeker people.

They went away, and I celebrated my triumph in a tent on the seashore of Byblos harbour. There I found a secure hiding place for Amen-of-the-Road and his property. But then the Prince of Byblos sent an abrupt message: "Get out of my harbour!"

My response was equally to the point.

"Where should I go? If you can find a ship that will carry me, I will return to Egypt. If not, I stay here."

I ended up wasting twenty-nine days in his harbour, while he sent daily messages ordering me to leave.

Then one day, while the Prince of Byblos was offering in his temple, the god possessed one of the boys in his entourage, and put him in a trance. The god spoke to the prince, through the voice of the boy.

"Bring the Egyptian god Amen-of-the-Road. And summon the envoy who escorts him. For he has been sent by the great god Amen-Re. It is Amen who has made him come to us."

That very day, just as the boy entered his trance, I had managed to track down a ship heading for Egypt. I had already loaded all my goods on board, and was waiting until nightfall so that I might load the god secretly, under cover of darkness. The next thing I knew, the harbour master was hurrying towards me.

"The prince orders you to stay, at least until tomorrow."

I couldn't believe my ears. "What! Aren't you the one who has been sending me daily messages telling me to go home. And now, just as I have found a ship that will carry me to Egypt, you are telling me to stay. Presumably when the ship has sailed, you will start ordering me to go home again! No, my friend, it is too late, I am going. Goodbye."

The harbour master rushed back to the Prince of Byblos, and he sent word to the captain of the ship, telling him to delay his departure.

The next morning the Prince of Byblos sent for me and I went to him, leaving the god resting in the tent on the seashore. I found the prince sitting in his imposing upper chamber, his back to the window. Behind him I could see the breaking waves of the great Syrian Sea.

I greeted the prince politely, as the occasion demanded.

"May the blessings of Amen be upon you."

He, however, did not feel the need for politeness. Abruptly, he started to question me.

"How long is it since you left Thebes, home of Amen?"

"I have been travelling for exactly five whole months to this day."

"But, if this is true, where is the letter from Amen-Re, King of the Gods, which details your mission? Where is the letter of authority from the High Priest of Amen?"

I explained all that had happened to me. "I gave the letter of authority to Smendes and Tantamen in Tanis."

This made him unaccountably angry. "Now, try to look at this matter from my point of view. You landed on my shore without any form of official validation. Where is the great ship that Smendes gave you to transport the wood? Where is its Syrian crew? Surely Egypt has her own fleet. Or, when Smendes entrusted you in the care of a Syrian sea-captain, did he intend the captain to murder you and throw your body overboard?"

Controlling my temper with some difficulty, I replied.

"It was an Egyptian ship, not a Syrian one. Those who sail under Smendes are Egyptian crews."

"I know what I am talking about. There are at least twenty ships here in my harbour that do business with Smendes."

I fell silent. Then the prince spoke again.

"Why exactly have you come here. What is your business?"

"I have come in search of timber for the great boat of Amen-Re, King of the Gods. Help me in my mission just as your father once helped Egypt's envoys, and your father's father before him."

The prince smiled at last, but it was not a kind smile.

"This, at least, I know to be true. And, of course, if you pay me properly I will indeed help you. My ancestors did supply wood to Egypt, but only after they had been properly rewarded. The King of Egypt sent six boats loaded with valuable Egyptian products, and they were unloaded into our warehouses. Then, and only then, he received his timber. But you have arrived empty handed and so deserve nothing."

To emphasise his point the prince called for the palace daybooks and had the relevant entries read to me; the entries mentioned a thousand *deben* of silver, and other precious goods. Then he spoke to me again, warming to his theme.

"If the King of Egypt were Lord of Byblos, and the Princes of Byblos merely his servants, he would never have sent silver and gold in payment - he would simply have taken what he needed for the service of Amen-Re. He paid my father and his father before him properly, as an equal. I am not your servant nor am I the servant of your master, and I should therefore be paid for my wood and my labour."

Then, perceiving my inability to pay as an insult to his nation, he went off into a rather alarming rant.

"Of course, obtaining timber is no trouble to me! I have only to shout out to the Lebanon, and the sky will open and the gods will drop the cut timber onto the beach. Give me the sails that you brought to move your ships loaded with timber back to Egypt. Give me the ropes that you brought to lash together the wood. Take your wood, and go!

"Ever since he placed Seth beside him, Amen has been able to thunder in the sky. We all know that Amen founded all the lands, and that he founded the land of Egypt first. We know that all crafts and learning started in Egypt, and travelled to Byblos. But now we have both crafts and learning in abundance - we require nothing more from your land. Yet you have arrived as a gift for us! So, tell me Wenamen, what exactly is the point of your pointless journey?"

"You are wrong! It is not a pointless journey. There is not a ship on the river that does not belong to Amen. He owns the sea and he even owns the Lebanon, although you claim it as your own land. Amen-Re, King of the Gods, told Herihor to send me on this quest, and he sent me with the Great God, Amen-of-the-Road. But you have made the Great God waste twenty-nine days in your harbour. Did you not realise that he was here, and why?

"Now you have the audacity to haggle with him, the owner of the Lebanon! You keep telling me that the Egyptian kings of old sent your ancestors gifts of silver and gold. Perhaps they did. But if they had been able to give the gift of life and health they would not have sent those paltry goods - they would have sent life and health instead.

"Amen-Re, King of the Gods, is the lord of life and health; it is he who was the lord of your fathers. They spent their lifetimes offering to Amen. You too are a servant of Amen. If you agree to do as he asks, you will live, prosper and be healthy. Your entire land will benefit. Do not covet the goods that belong to Amen-Re, King of the Gods. Instead send your scribe to me so that I may write to Smendes and Tantamen, the two pillars that Amen has set up in the north of his land. They will send you whatever payment you think necessary. I will explain matters to them; I will ask them to send you payment until I return to the south of Egypt, then my master Herihor will refund their expenses."

The Prince of Byblos gave my letter to his messenger, and he loaded the ship with the keel piece, the bow, the stern plus four great logs - a total of seven hewn logs - and he sent them to Egypt. I remained in Syria. The messenger returned to me in the first month of winter. Smendes and Tantamen had not let me down. Here is a list of the goods that they sent:

> Gold jars - 4
> Gold vessels - 1
> Silver bowls - 5
> Garments made from fine royal linen - 10
> Sheets of fine linen - 10
> Smooth linen mats 500
> Ox hides - 500
> Ropes - 500
> Sacks of lentils - 20
> Baskets of fish - 30

In addition the queen sent me a personal gift of five fine linen garments, five fine linen covers, one sack of lentils and five sacks of fish.

The sight of so many precious goods galvanised the Prince of Byblos. Three hundred men and three hundred oxen set to work under the supervision of his personally chosen officials. They felled the timber that I needed, and it lay on the ground throughout the winter. In the third month of summer the logs were dragged to the seashore. The prince went to inspect them, and he summoned me. But when I had been ushered into his presence, an unfortunate thing happened. The shadow of his fan fell across me. Seeing this Penamen, Egyptian butler to the Prince of Byblos, made a big fuss.

"The shadow of the King of Egypt, your lord, has fallen on you."

But the prince grew angry with Penamen, and told him to leave me alone.

As I stood before the Prince of Byblos, he spoke to me: "Look, I have now done the same business with you that my father and grandfather did in the past, although you have not treated me as well as they were treated. The last of your timber has now been cut, and lies ready. Do as I wish, and load it onto your ship, for it has been given to you. But do not look at the terror of the sea. For if you look at the terror of the sea, you will see my very own terror. You should note that I have not treated you in the same way that the envoys sent by Khaemwaset were treated. They spent seventeen years in this land, and eventually died here."

And turning to his butler, he ordered him to take me to the place where the envoys of Khaemwaset were buried so that I might see just how my unfortunate compatriots had fared.

"Do not make me see this terrible thing," I cried, horrified. "The envoys sent by Khaemwaset were mere men, just as Khaemwaset himself was a mere man. I am not one of his envoys, and you can't tell me what to do. I may be a mortal envoy, but I am sent by a great god. You should rejoice at my coming and have a magnificent stela carved in celebration. And on it you should proclaim, for all to read:

Amen-Re, King of the Gods, sent his divine messenger Amen-of-the-Road, and his mortal messenger Wenamen, to my land in search of the timber needed to build the riverboat of the great god Amen-Re. I felled the trees, and I loaded the logs onto the ships that I had supplied. I sent the wood to Egypt - and in exchange I asked that Amen grant me an extra fifty years of life beyond that which the fates had planned.

"Then, if it should ever happen that another Egyptian envoy comes to your land and he is able to read your stela, you will receive the water of the west like the gods who dwell there."

The prince spoke to me again, thanking me with some irony for my unasked-for advice. And I assured him that all my debts to him would be repaid in full when I, and the ships, reached Thebes.

I went down to the seashore, where the logs lay ready and waiting. At last it seemed that my long mission was over and I could return home. But then I saw to my horror that eleven Tjeker ships had docked, and their sailors were roaming the shore looking for me.

"There he is! Arrest him! Under no circumstances allow his ship to sail for Egypt!"

There was nothing I could do to escape. I would never leave Byblos. I would never see my homeland again. I sat down and wept on the shore.

The scribe of the Prince of Byblos came to me, concerned that I was weeping on what should have been a happy occasion. He asked me what was wrong. And I told him of my sorrow at being stranded far from home.

"Look into the sky - can you see the birds migrating? I have lived here for so long that I have already seen them fly twice to Egypt, and now am forced to watch as they journey north again to the cooler lands. When will I ever be able to fly away? Look, can't you see, those men have come to arrest me."

The scribe went straight to the prince and told him of this new development. And the prince, moved to tears by my words, sent the scribe back to me bringing two jugs of wine and a sheep. He also sent Tentne, a famous Egyptian singer who worked at his court, and he told her to sing me cheerful songs that would take my mind off my problems. He sent a message with the scribe.

"Eat, drink and be merry if you can, Wenamen. Don't worry about your situation. For tomorrow I will pronounce judgement on your case."

In the morning Tjeker-Baal, Prince of Byblos, summoned his court. He questioned the Tjeker closely: "Why have you come here? What exactly do you want?"

"We demand the right to confiscate the ships that you are sending to Egypt with our enemy."

The prince considered for a moment, then reached his decision.

"I cannot allow this to happen on my land. I cannot be responsible for arresting the envoy of the Great God Amen-Re. I will send the envoy off to sea, and you must arrest him there."

Hearing this, my heart sank. The prince made me board my ship, and I sailed from the harbour. The strong wind drove me towards Cyprus, and there I landed.

I had gone from a bad situation to a worse one. The townspeople rushed out of their houses, determined to kill me. But I forced my way into the presence of Hatiba, their princess. I ran to her as she left her palace and, in desperate fear for my life, asked if anyone could translate my words so that I might plead my case. Most fortunately, there was a man in the crowd who could speak Egyptian very well. And so I was able to speak to the good lady.

"Madam, living at Thebes, home of the Great God Amen, I have heard many stories of injustices committed in other lands. But I never heard that the land of Cyprus was unjust. Now prove to me that your land is indeed a just one."

She looked at me in surprise. "What do you mean by that? Explain yourself, foreigner."

And so I spoke at length. "The great sea raged, and the strong wind blew me to your land against my will. Will you really allow your people to kill me, the envoy of Amen? Your people have determined that they will never let me go - they may well kill me. But think about this. If they kill the sailors from Byblos who crew my ship, the Prince of Byblos will hunt down ten of your ships, and kill their crews in revenge."

Hatiba saw the sense of my words. She summoned the people to her, and reprimanded them. Then she spoke to me "Stay the night, Wenamen...."

COMMENTARY ON
THE VOYAGE OF WENAMEN

Just one version of *The Voyage of Wenamen* (Papyrus Moscow 120) has survived. Unfortunately the beginning of the story has significant gaps, and its end is missing. The papyrus has been dated to the late 20th or early 21st Dynasty. It is set during the reign of Ramesses XI, and tells of a trading mission sent from Thebes to buy wood from the Lebanon. This should have been a simple transaction - her shortage of tall trees meant that Egypt had been importing wood for many centuries. But Wenamen lives in turbulent times. The once glorious New Kingdom is rapidly nearing its end, the empire has vanished, and Egypt has little or no influence over her neighbours who feel free to demand cash in advance for their goods and services.

Back home things are no better. Ramesses XI, last of the Ramesside rulers, is King of Egypt in name only. True power is shared between two influential men. In the south there is Herihor, High Priest of Amen, based at Thebes. In the north there is Smendes, based at the eastern Delta city of Tanis. Smendes will later become the first king of the 21st Dynasty.

Experts are divided over the authenticity of this story - is it an accurate, official report of a genuine trade mission, or is it a work of fiction set in a real historical time - the New Kingdom equivalent of *Sinuhe*? Could it even be both - a fictionalised account based on a real document? Certainly Herihor does claim, on the wall of the Khonsu Temple at Karnak, that he built a boat for Amen "from Lebanese wood, decorated with gold throughout". While at first sight the story reads like a lengthy administrative document submitted by an inept, and unduly pompous official with a strong devotion to Amen, the bizarre sequence of events, the lengthy conversations reported word for word and the (we assume) deliberate use of irony suggest that it may be fiction.

As a southerner, Wenamen dates the key events of his adventure using the "Renaissance Era" dates introduced by Herihor. Year 5 mentioned by Wenamen therefore equates to Year 23 of Ramesses XI. But the dates he gives have no chronological logic. I have amended his first date, "day 16 of the fourth month of summer, Year 5" so that it reads "second month of summer" - this makes better sense if Wenamen is to stay at Tanis "until the fourth month of summer". Similarly, it is likely that Wenamen sails down to the great Syrian Sea on the "first day of the first month of the inundation" rather than the "first day of the first month of summer".

Smendes waves Wenamen off on a ship whose captain bears the Syrian name Mengebet. The crew, too, are likely to be Syrian. But, as Wenamen himself later stresses, the ship belongs to, or has been hired by, Smendes, and should therefore be classed as an Egyptian vessel. It is unfortunate that Wenamen's precious belongings - the "money" brought to pay for the wood needed for the god's boat - are taken by a member of his own crew. This heinous crime is committed while Wenamen is moored at Dor, a Palestinian port controlled by the Tjeker, one of a loose confederation of eastern Mediterranean peoples known as the "Sea People". Having tried, and failed, to invade Egypt during the reign of Ramesses III, the Sea People have settled along the Palestinian coast where they pose a subdued but ever-present threat to Egypt.

Wenamen asks Beder, Prince of Dor, to replace the goods that, as he points out, have been stolen not from him personally but from all the people involved in the trade chain - Amen, Smendes, Herihor, Weret (Prince of Tyre?), Mekmer (Prince of Sidon?) and Tjeker-Baal, Prince of Byblos. Wenamen is no *Talkative Peasant*; he is not prepared to wait indefinitely for justice. As Beder is unwilling to take responsibility for the loss Wenamen, perhaps encouraged by Beder, takes matters into his own hands by confiscating 30 *deben* of silver from a Tjeker ship just outside Byblos harbour. The *deben* was a measure of valuable metal (copper, silver or gold). Small-scale theft, of course, can only be a temporary solution to Wenamen's problem, and ultimately it gets him further into trouble.

Wenamen is accompanied, and protected, on his adventure by a small portable god, Amen-of-the-Road. This smaller Amen is kept hidden, and Tjeker-Baal of Byblos is at first unaware of his existence. It is left to his own Canaanite god to reveal the presence of Amen-of-the-Road in Byblos.

Only now is Wenamen summoned to his audience chamber. Tjeker-Baal is faced with an impoverished, document-less envoy who has committed an act of piracy and who is now demanding expensive wood on the grounds that it has been supplied to his country in the past. The two embark on a lengthy and not always serious or productive discussion of the problem. Tjeker-Baal is not over-impressed by Wenamen's argument that he should provide goods and services for Amen in exchange for a vague promise of a long, healthy life - he prefers money. Whether or not Wenamen truly believes he is making a good offer, or whether he is attempting the cynical exploitation of a gullible foreigner, we do not know.

Wenamen's case is not helped by his barely-concealed assumption that Egypt is entitled to take whatever she wants. Tjeker-Baal's response, however, is difficult for us to understand unless he is employing a deep irony: "Of course you don't have to pay - after all there is no work involved. I merely have to call out loud and the wood miraculously appears". Egypt - or Amen - is in no position to enforce any request for free wood. Wenamen is forced to write to Smendes for a loan that will be repaid by Herihor.

We do not know who Khaemwaset is, although it is assumed that he is a late Ramesside official charged with obtaining yet more wood. Wenamen refuses to visit the graves of the unfortunate envoys - instead he recommends that Tjeker-Baal sets up a stela to commemorate his own visit.

ONE HYMN

If Amenhotep IV had been content merely to claim for his god a place among the other gods of Egypt he might have gone down to his grave in peace.

James Baikie, *The Amarna Age*, 1926

16

THE GREAT HYMN TO THE ATEN

Glorious, you rise on the horizon of heaven,
O living Aten, creator of life.
Dawning on the eastern horizon,
You flood every land with your perfect light.
You are dazzling, wonderful and radiant, high over every land.
Your rays embrace all the lands,
All the lands that you have made.
You are Re and so you reach their borders,
Defining them for your beloved son.
Though you are far away, your rays light the earth.
Though you are seen, your movement is not.

When you set on the western horizon
The land grows dark, as if death had come.
Dark night must be spent asleep in a bedroom with a
covered head,
One eye cannot see the other.
In the dark no one would notice
If the possessions under their heads were stolen.
At night every lion comes out from its den,
And every serpent bites.
Darkness falls and the earth is hushed,
Because its maker rests on the horizon.

But the earth lights up when you rise from the horizon,
Shining bright, the Aten of the day.
You banish the darkness as you unsheathe your rays.
The Two Lands celebrate,
They grow lively and aroused.
You have awakened the people who,
With bodies cleansed and clothing donned,
Raise their arms to praise your rising.

Now the whole land starts to work.
Cattle graze on their fodder,
Trees and plants grow.
Birds fly off from their nests,
Their wings stretched in praise of your spirit.
The flocks gambol in the fields,
And everything that flies and perches
Lives because you have dawned for them.
Ships sail to the north and to the south,
Roads open at your rising.
The fish in the river leap before you,
For your rays reach the middle of the sea.

You make the seed grow in women
And create mankind from sperm.
You feed the son in his mother's womb,
You comfort him and stop his tears.
You are the nurse within the womb,
Who gives breath to all that he has made.
On the day the baby is born, when he takes his first
breath,
You open his mouth and supply all his needs.
When the chick in the egg chirps in his shell,
You give him the breath to live.
When his time has come to break free

He hatches and proclaims his birth.
Walking on his legs he leaves the shell.

You do so many things,
Things that are hidden from my view.
O sole god, you are without compare.
You created the world as you desired,
And you created it alone.
All the people, all the cattle, all the flocks,
Everything that walks with its feet on the earth,
And everything that flies with its wings in the air.
Northern Asia, southern Africa,
The land of Egypt herself.
You have set every man in his place,
And you have met his needs.
Everyone has his food,
Everyone has his allotted life span.
Tongues vary in their speech,
And characters and skins also vary,
For you have differentiated mankind.

You created the Nile in the Netherworld.
You bring him forth at your will,
To feed the people
That you made for yourself.
Master of all, you toil for them.
Lord of all lands, you shine for them.
For them the daytime Aten dawns,
Glorious and great.

You make all distant lands live.
For you have made a heavenly Nile come down for them,
To make waves on the mountains like the sea,
To water the fields of their towns.

O Lord of eternity,
How excellent are your designs.
A Nile from heaven for the foreigners,
And all their creatures that walk the lands.
And a Nile for Egypt springing from the Netherworld.

Your rays suckle every field.
When you shine they live, and they grow for you.
You made the seasons to nurture all you made
Winter to cool them and Summer that they may feel you.

You made a distant sky,
In which you might shine.
From there you see everything that you have made.
There you are alone,
Shining as the Living Aten.
Risen, dazzling, far away and yet near by.
You have manifested yourself many times.
Towns, villages, fields, roads and waterways;
Every eye sees you upon them,
For you are the Aten of the daytime...

You are my beloved.
No other knows you as I do,
Only your son Neferkheperure Waenre.
You have taught me of your plans and your power.
The creatures of the earth exist in your hand as you have
made them
When you dawn they live, when you set they die.
You are a lifetime; it is by you that men live.
Eyes may look upon your beauty until you set,
But when you go down in the west all work must cease.
You who rise and make everything grow
For the king, and those who hurry on foot.

You raise them up for the son who came forth from your body, the King of Upper and Lower Egypt, Living in Maat, the Lord of the Two Lands Neferkheperure Waenre, son of Re, living in Truth, Lord of the glorious appearings, Akhenaten, the long-lived.

And for the King's Great Wife whom he loves, the Mistress of the Two Lands, Neferneferuaten-Nefertiti, may she live and flourish forever and ever.

COMMENTARY ON
THE GREAT HYMN TO THE ATEN

The Great Hymn to the Aten was carved on the east wall of the unfinished Amarna tomb of the courtier Ay, father-in-law of the unorthodox 18th Dynasty ruler Akhenaten. It is one of three prayers in this tomb directed towards Akhenaten and his god, and is presented beneath a damaged scene showing the royal family worshipping the Aten. *The Great Hymn* is presumed to have been written by the king himself. It is not an innovative piece of work - there had been earlier hymns praising the sun god - but it has a poetic beauty and an unexpected monotheistic element which have encouraged comparisons with Psalm 104, which was written some five hundred years later:

> *Bless the Lord, O my soul, O lord my God, thou art very great; thou art clothed with honour and majesty. Who coverest thyself with light as with a garment: who stretchest out the heavens like a curtain... Thou makest darkness, and it is night: wherein all the beasts of the forest do creep forth. The young lions roar after their prey, and seek their meat from God. The sun ariseth, and they gather themselves together, and lay them down in their dens...*

Akhenaten is often described, rather lazily, as the "heretic pharaoh". Certainly his reign - the Amarna period - was a time of intense theological confusion for Egypt's elite. Within five years of his accession Akhenaten had banned the vast majority of the old gods and replaced them with the Aten; a faceless sun disk who hovered in the sky above the king and queen, and whose many rays ended in small hands capable of grasping the *ankh*, symbol of life.

The ordinary people, who had never been involved in the worship of the state gods, were more or less free to believe what they wished. But the courtiers had to be seen to follow their king - they had to become devotees of the sun god. As the old temples closed their gates the royal court left Thebes and moved to Amarna (ancient Akhetaten), a purpose-built city in the Middle Egyptian desert, dedicated to the worship of the Aten. Here Ay and his fellow courtiers were forced to live increasingly isolated lives, deprived not only of their gods but also of their houses and even their ancestral tombs. Armed soldiers guarded the boundaries of the new city. Today, some 3,000 years after the last patrol left the barracks, we can still see the paths worn by their marching feet. We cannot, of course, tell whether such an obvious military presence was needed to protect Amarna against invasion, or whether it was needed to persuade the citizens to stay.

All this must have come as a massive shock to the Egyptians, a people so conservative that their art, politics, religion, and, as far as we can tell, thought processes, had remained more or less constant for centuries. Everyone knew that the king, as the one mortal able to communicate with the gods, was charged with the maintenance of *maat* - the essential force which, since the beginning of time, had kept chaos at bay. He had the awful responsibility of pleasing the capricious gods who would hold back *isfet* and protect Egypt. Now, at a stroke, the old certainties had been swept away. Akhenaten had most publicly declared the old gods impotent - they could no longer protect Egypt. In their place the newly vulnerable land was left with a faceless, characterless disk and an eccentric king who was not prepared to conform to the traditions of kingship.

The Aten was a highly visible yet very impersonal god. It was an asexual divinity, symbolising the light of the sun rather than the sun itself, and it shone down exclusively on the royal family, leaving less exalted beings to seek religious comfort elsewhere. Now there was no hope of an afterlife alongside Osiris in the Field of Reeds. It was official - Osiris no longer existed. Instead Ay had to hope that his soul would survive within his dark tomb. Here he could worship the king, his family and his god, for all eternity.

However, we should not be misled by the monotheistic element discernible in *The Great Hymn*. The Aten was never Egypt's only god. Some of the old solar deities, Re and Maat being the most obvious examples, survived the purge to play their own parts in the cult of the Aten. At the same time Akhenaten, his queen Nefertiti and their children were offered to the people as replacements for their missing gods. Akhenaten was the son of Re and, as the Aten was the visible, physical aspect of Re, he became the earthly manifestation of the sun god. As the "Beautiful Child of the Disk" he was the sole interpreter standing between the Aten and his people. Nefertiti was his consort, their children living symbols of the king's fertility.

The king had abandoned his given name, Amenhotep ("Amen is Satisfied"), soon after the start of his reign because it made reference to the hated god of Thebes. His chosen name, Akhenaten, means "Living Spirit of the Aten", while his throne name, Neferkheperure Waenre, translates as "The Transformations of Re are Perfect, the Unique One of Re". Akhenaten's beautiful wife Nefertiti was more formally known as Neferneferuaten Nefertiti, or "Beautiful are the Beauties of the Aten, A Beautiful Woman has Come".

Ay, whose name has no specific meaning, outlived Akhenaten and Nefertiti to become King of Egypt, ruling for four years after Tutankhamen's untimely death. All the Amarna tombs were abandoned, along with the city, when Tutankhamen restored the old religion and moved the court back to Thebes. Both Tutankhamen and Ay would be buried in the Valley of the Kings. Both, inextricably linked to the heresies of the Amarna age, would be omitted from the official Egyptian king lists.

BIBLIOGRAPHY AND FURTHER READING

A vast number of books has been published examining all aspects of Egyptian literature and writings. Here I have given preference to books and more accessible articles published in English. This reading list is, however, just a starting point; all of these works provide extensive bibliographies. Happy reading!

TRANSLATIONS AND RETELLINGS OF ANCIENT TEXTS

The earlier accounts, although possessing great literary charm, are nowhere near as accurate as the later works cited and should not be relied on as accurate translations.

Baikie, J. (1925), *Egyptian Papyri and Papyrus-Hunting*, London.
Erman, A. (1927), *The Literature of the Ancient Egyptians*, translated by A.M. Blackman, London. (Also published as *Ancient Egyptians: a sourcebook of their writings*, New York 1966)
Foster, J.L. (1992), *Echoes of Egyptian Voices: an Anthology of Ancient Egyptian Poetry*, Norman and London.
Kitchen, K.A. (1996), *Ramesside Inscriptions Translated and Annotated 2: Ramesses II Royal Inscriptions*, Oxford.
Kitchen, K.A. (1999), *Poetry of Ancient Egypt*, Jonsered.
Lichtheim, M. (1973), *Ancient Egyptian Literature I: The Old and*

Middle Kingdoms, Berkeley and London.

Lichtheim, M. (1976), *Ancient Egyptian Literature II: The New Kingdom*, Berkeley and London.

Mackenzie, D.A. (1913), *Egyptian Myth and Legend*, London.

Parkinson, R.B. (1991), *Voices From Ancient Egypt: an Anthology of Middle Kingdom Writings*, London.

Parkinson, R.B. (1997), *The Tale of Sinuhe and Other Ancient Egyptian Poems 1940-1640 BC*, Oxford.

Pritchard, J.B. (ed.) (1969), *Ancient Near Eastern Texts Relating to the New Testament*, 3rd Edition, Princeton.

Simpson, W.K. (ed.) (2003), *The Literature of Ancient Egypt: an Anthology of Stories, Instructions, Stelae, Autobiographies, and Poetry*, 3rd Edition, New Haven and London.

BACKGROUND READING

Baines, J. and Eyre, C.J. (1983), Four Notes on Literacy, *Göttinger Miszellen* 61: 65-96.

Hart, G. (2003), *Egyptian Myths*, London. (Published both as an individual title and as part of a compilation volume entitled *World of Myths*)

Loprieno, A. (ed.) (1996), *Ancient Egyptian Literature: History and Form*, Leiden, New York and Köln.

Parkinson, R.B. and Quirke, S. (1995), *Papyrus*, London.

Redford, D.B (editor in chief) (2001), *The Oxford Encyclopaedia of Ancient Egypt*, 3 volumes, Oxford.

Snape, S. (1997), *Decoding the Stones*, London.

TALES OF GODS AND GODDESSES

Allen, J.R. (1988), *Genesis in Egypt: the Philosophy of Ancient Egyptian Creation Accounts*, New Haven.

Baines, J. (1991), Egyptian Myth and Discourse: Myths, Gods and the Early Written and Iconographic Record, *Journal of Near Eastern Studies* 50: 81-105.

Griffiths, J.G. (1970), *Plutarch's De Iside et Osiride*, Cardiff.

Hornung, E. (1983), *Conceptions of God in Ancient Egypt: the One and the Many*, London.

Quirke, S. (1992), *Ancient Egyptian Religion*, London.

Quirke, S. (2001), *The Cult of Ra: Sun Worship in Ancient Egypt*, London.

Watterson, B (1984, reprinted 1996), *The Gods of Ancient Egypt*, London and Gloucestershire.

Wilkinson, R.H. (2003), *The Complete Gods and Goddesses of Ancient Egypt*, London.

TALES OF MEN

Baines, J. (1982), Interpreting Sinuhe, *Journal of Egyptian Archaeology* 68: 31-44.

Baines, J. (1990), Interpreting the Story of the Shipwrecked Sailor, *Journal of Egyptian Archaeology* 76: 55-72.

Eyre, C.J. (1976), Fate, Crocodiles and Judgement of the Dead: Some Mythological Allusions in Egyptian Literature, *Studien zur Altägyptischen Kultur* 4: 103-14.

Eyre, C.J. (1992), Yet Again the Wax Crocodile, *Journal of Egyptian Archaeology* 78: 280-1.

Hollis, S.T (1990), *The Ancient Egyptian "Tale of Two Brothers": the oldest fairy tale in the World*, Norman.

Manniche, L. (1981), *The Prince Who Knew his Fate: an Ancient Egyptian Tale Translated from Hieroglyphs and Illustrated*, New York.

Parkinson, R.B. (1991), *The Tale of the Eloquent Peasant*, Oxford.

Parkinson, R.B. (2002), *Poetry and Culture in Middle Kingdom Egypt: a Dark Side to Perfection*, London and New York.

Tyldesley, J.A. (2000), *Judgement of the Pharaoh: Crime and Punishment in Ancient Egypt*, London.

Wettengel, W. (2003), *Die Erzahlung von den beiden Brudern*, Fribourg.

TRUE STORIES

Eyre, C.J. (1999), Irony in the Story of Wenamun: the Politics of Religion in the 21st Dynasty, in J. Assmann and E. Blumenthal (eds) *Literatur und Politik im Pharaonischen und Ptolemäischen Ägypten*, Institut Français d'Archéologie Orientale 127: 235-252.

Kitchen, K.A. (1982), *Pharaoh Triumphant: the Life and Times of Ramesses II*, Warminster.

Kitchen, K.A. (1999*), Ramesside Royal Inscriptions Translated and Annotated 2: Notes and Comments*, Oxford.

Lichtheim, M. (1988), *Ancient Egyptian Autobiographies Chiefly of the Middle Kingdom: a Study and an Anthology*, Göttingen.

Tyldesley, J.A. (2000), *Ramesses, Egypt's Greatest Pharaoh*, London.

ONE HYMN

Aldred, C. (1988), *Akhenaten; King of Egypt*, London.

Monserrat, D. (2000), *Akhenaten: History Fantasy and Ancient Egypt*, London.

Redford, D.B. (1984), *Akhenaten: the Heretic King*, Princeton.

Reeves, N. (2001), *Akhenaten: Egypt's False Prophet*, London.

Tyldesley, J.A. (1998), *Nefertiti: Egypt's Sun Queen*, London.

INDEX OF PEOPLE AND PLACES